Hidden Messages

Hidden Messages

Representation and Resistance in Andean Colonial Drama

Raquel Chang-Rodríguez

Lewisburg
Bucknell University Press
London: Associated University Presses

© 1999 by Associated University Presses, Inc.

All rights reserved. Authorization to photocopy items for internal or personal use, or the internal or personal use of specific clients, is granted by the copyright owner, provided that a base fee of $10.00, plus eight cents per page, per copy is paid directly to the Copyright Clearance Center, 222 Rosewood Drive, Danvers, Massachusetts 01923. [0-8387-5421-X/99 $10.00+8¢ pp, pc.]

Associated University Presses
440 Forsgate Drive
Cranbury, NJ 08512

Associated University Presses
16 Barter Street
London WC1A 2AH, England

Associated University Presses
P.O. Box 338, Port Credit
Mississauga, Ontario
Canada L5G 4L8

The paper used in this publication meets the requirements of the American National Standard for Permanence of Paper for Printed Library Materials Z39.48-1984.

Library of Congress Cataloging-in-Publication Data

Chang-Rodríguez, Raquel.
    Hidden messages : representation and resistance in Andean colonial drama / Raquel Chang-Rodríguez.
       p.   cm.
    Includes bibliographical references (p.   ) and index.
    ISBN 0-8387-5421-X (alk. paper)
    1. Peruvian drama—History and criticism. 2. Quechua drama—History and criticism. 3. Indians of South America—First contact with Europeans I. Title.
PQ8385.C43   1999
862—dc21   98-47707
                                                                                                                    CIP

PRINTED IN THE UNITED STATES OF AMERICA

Contents

List of Illustrations	9
Acknowledgments	11
Introduction	15
1. Movable Meanings: Evangelization, Literacy and Missionary Theater	21
2. Historical and Cultural Contentions in *Tragedia del fin de Atahualpa*	36
3. The Interface of Religious and Scenic Arts in the Quechua Play *Usca Paucar*	59
4. Expanding Baroque Boundaries in *Amar su propia muerte* by Juan de Espinosa Medrano	84
5. Trespassing on Tradition: Francisco del Castillo's *La Conquista del Perú*	98
Conclusion	117
Notes	119
Bibliography	129
Index	141

To Gabriella de Beer and Louis Levine in friendship.

>   Si dicen que del joyero
> Tome la joya mejor,
> Tomo a un amigo sincero
> Y pongo a un lado el amor.
>
>   —José Martí, *Versos sencillos*

List of Illustrations

Title page of *Doctrina cristiana muy útil y necesaria* (1578), attributed to Francisco de Pareja.   26

Teaching the Ten Commandments. *Doctrina cristiana muy útil y necesaria* (1578), attributed to Francisco de Pareja.   27

Detail of a Franciscan friar preaching the Gospel. *Doctrina cristiana muy útil y necesaria* (1578), attributed to Francisco de Pareja.   28

The meeting of Pizarro, Almagro, Felipillo, Valverde, and Atahualpa in Cajamarca (Guaman Poma [1615] 2:386).   37

The ship of the "discovery" (Guaman Poma [1615] 1:46).   42

The "beheading" of Atahualpa (Guaman Poma [1615] 2:392).   44

Tupac Amaru I carried in chains by Martín García de Loyola (Guaman Poma [1615] 2:451).   45

The death of the last Inca king at the square of Cuzco (Guaman Poma [1615] 2:453).   46

Viceroy Toledo after his interview with Philip II of Spain (Guaman Poma [1615] 2:460).   57

Manco Inca attempts to burn the church during his rebellion against Spanish rule (Guaman Poma [1615] 2:402).   65

The Apostle Saint James helping the conquistadors during the seige of Cuzco. (Guaman Poma [1615] 2:406).   66

The appearance of the Virgin Mary during the siege of Cuzco. (Guaman Poma [1615] 2:404).   67

Our Lady of Copacabana as depicted by Francisco de Bejarano in the title page of *Santuario de Copacabana* (1641) by Fernando de Valverde.   69

The Virgin of Pomata, 1675. Anonymous. 70

Devout couple saying the rosary before an image of
Christ on the cross (Guaman Poma [1615] 2:835). 72

An Indian saying the rosary before an image of the Virgin
(Guaman Poma [1615] 2:847). 73

Virgin of Copacabana—Our Lady of the Peña de Francia
surrounded by a rosary (Guaman Poma [1615] 2:841). 74

Archangel Saint Michael triumphs over Satan (late
seventeenth century?), Church of San Juan Bautista,
Huallabamba, Peru. 77

Military Archangel (late seventeenth century?), Parochial
Church of Maras, Peru. 78

Standard-bearer Archangel (late seventeenth century?),
Parochial Church of Maras, Peru. 79

Candía, the Greek artilleryman, in an imaginary
conversation with Inca Huayna Capac (Guaman Poma
[1615] 2:371). 103

Inca Huayna Capac with the symbols of his authority
(Guaman Poma [1615] 1:112). 106

The mummified body of Huayna Capac carried on a litter
to Cuzco (Guaman Poma [1615] 2:379). 107

The rebel leader Rumiñagüi (Guaman Poma [1615] 1:165). 115

Acknowledgments

I WISH FIRST TO GIVE SPECIAL THANKS TO MY GENEROUS AND LOYAL friends Gabriella de Beer and Frederick Luciani for reading an earlier version of the manuscript and offering many helpful suggestions. For useful insights during the last stage of the preparation of this project, my thanks to Julie G. Johnson. I am grateful to Julio Noriega Bernuy for reviewing my translations from Quechua to English. I would like to express my appreciation to several friends and colleagues for encouraging me to complete this book and for offering the support that enabled me to do it: Ottavio Di Camillo, Luis Rafael Sánchez, and Eve Sourian. My thanks to the staff of the Morris Raphael Cohen Library of The City College of New York (CCNY) and of the Mina Rees Library of the Graduate School and University Center of the City University of New York (CUNY) for their assistance, particularly to Julio Rosario and Mark Padnos for their help in searches and inter-library loan requests. I am grateful to John O'Neill for preparing the computerized version of the manuscript for publication. I thank Gregory Clingham, director of Bucknell University Press, for his enthusiastic support.

My interest in theater goes back to the days when I was a graduate student and, in particular, to a memorable class on Golden Age drama taught by Alexander A. Parker. Later, the Spanish American angle of this interest was nurtured by many discussions with José Juan Arrom. In the last years I have shared numerous conversations on colonial art, literature and history that have enriched my understanding of these fields with Rolena Adorno, Trinidad Barrera, Guadalupe Fernández Ariza, Teresa Gisbert, José Carlos González Boixo, Pedro Guibovich, Oswaldo Holguín Callo, Pedro Lasarte, Asunción Lavrin, José Antonio Mazzotti, Carmen de Mora, Mabel Moraña, Mariana Mould de

Pease, José Antonio Rodríguez, Alberto Sandoval, Georgina Sabat de Rivers, Elias Rivers, Franklin Pease G. Y., Enrique Pupo-Walker, Concepción Reverte Bernal, Sonia Rose, Carmen Ruiz Barrionuevo and the late lamented Antonio Cornejo Polar.

The initial research for this project was supported in part by a grant from the Professional Staff Congress-City University of New York Research Foundation and The Program for Cultural Cooperation Between Spain's Ministry of Culture and United States Universities, which I gratefully acknowledge. I wish to express my appreciation to Martin Tamny, Dean of Humanities and Arts at The City College of the City University of New York, for his constant encouragement and unfailing support of my research.

I thank the following persons and institutions for the permissions granted to publish the following materials:

Illustrations. José A. Sánchez Paso, Ediciones de la Universidad de Salamanca, for Francisco de Pareja, *Doctrina cristiana muy útil y necesaria*. Edición y estudio al cuidado de Luis Resines. Salamanca: Ediciones de la Universidad de Salamanca, 1990. John V. Murra and Rolena Adorno, eds. Felipe Guaman Poma de Ayala. *Primer nueva corónica y buen gobierno*, 3 vols. (Mexico: Siglo XXI, 1980). Anonymous, *Our Lady of Pomata* (c. 1675), courtesy of The Brooklyn Museum of Art, Museum Expedition 1941, Frank L. Babbott Fund 41.1275.177. Francisco de Bejarano, woodcut of *Nuestra Señora de Copacabana* in *Santuario de Nuestra Señora de Copacabana* (1641) by Fernando de Valverde, courtesy of the John Carter Brown Library at Brown University. Anonymous, *Archangel Saint Michael triumphs over Satan*, Church of San Juan Bautista, Huallabamba, Peru. Anonymous, *Military Archangel* and Anonymous, *Standard Bearer Archangel*, Parochial Church of Maras, Peru, courtesy of Arzobispado del Cuzco, Peru, and World Monuments Fund (New York).

Journals and Collections. Earlier versions of chapter 1 appeared in "Convergencias y divergencias culturales: indígenas y europeos en la 'biblioteca amerciana.'" *Asedios a la heterogeneidad cultural. Libro de homenaje a Antonio Cornejo Polar*. Eds. José A. Mazzotti y U. Juan Zevallos Aguilar. Ann Arbor: Asociación Internacional de Peruanistas, 1996. 121–34. Of chapter 2 in "Cultural Resistance in the Andes and Its Depiction in *Atau Wallpaj P' uchukakuyninpa Wankan* or *Tragedy of Atahualpa's Death.*" In *Coded Encounters.* Eds. Francisco Javier Cevallos-Candau et al. Amherst: University of Massachusetts Press, 1994. 11–34; and "El renacimiento del Inca." *Discursos sobre la "invención" de América.* Ed. Iris Zavala. Amsterdam: Rodopi, 1992. 73–99. Of chapter 3 in "Salvación y sumisión en el *Usca Paucar,* un drama quechua colonial." Ed. Mercedes López Baralt. *Revista de Estudios Hispánicos* 19 (1992): 357–82. Of chapter 4 in "La subversión del barroco en *Amar su propia muerte* de Juan de Espinosa Medrano." *Relecturas del barroco de Indias.* Ed. Mabel Moraña. Hanover, N.H.: Ediciones del Norte, 1994. 117–47. Versions of chapters 2, 3 and 4 have appeared in my *El discurso disidente* (Lima: Pontificia Universidad Católica del Perú, 1991). Of chapter 5 in "Entre la tradición colonial y la ruptura ilustrada: *La conquista del Perú* de fray Francisco del Castillo." *Crítica y descolonización: el sujeto colonial en la cultura latinoamericana.* Eds. Lúcia Helena Costigan and Beatriz González Stephan. Caracas-Columbus: "Equinoccio", Academia Nacional de la Historia, Universidad Simón Bolívar and The Ohio State University, 1992. 467–89.

My special thanks to Mr. Julien Yoseloff, Director, Associated University Presses, and the following members of his staff: Jean Harvie, Melody Sadighi and Brian J. Haskell, Production Editors, Ellen Kazar, Art Director, Michael Koy and Christine A. Retz, Managing Editors, for their assistance in the different stages of the production of this book.

Introduction

DURING THE COLONIAL PERIOD IN SPANISH AMERICA, THEATER and sermons were the only means of mass communication with a public of different cultural and ethnic heritages. The missionaries of the religious orders were the first to realize the effectiveness of the stage for cross-cultural communication. In their zeal to convert the Indian population, they searched for the most efficient method to bring Catholic dogma to the American neophytes. Pantomime and decorations were incorporated into the representation of sacred history, lives of saints, and the mysteries of the faith as a way to compensate for the inadequacy of verbal communication. With the assistance, first of Indian informants, and later of missionary priests that had mastered Amerindian languages, the translation of Spanish religious plays into these languages promptly began. In the process of translation and representation, such foreign plays were often refashioned. They were modified and enriched by the different interpretations of the heterogeneous public and by the particular colonial juncture in which they were embedded.

Later the colonial Spanish public, which was familiar with the staging of Peninsular plays, tried every way possible to bring the popular Golden Age dramas and plays to America. The arrival and staging of plays by the admired Spanish masters in fact helped to increase the prestige that theater had in America, and to heighten the enjoyment and the concerns that spectators experienced when attending performances. At the same time, the popularity of these performances motivated writers living in the Spanish Indies to try their hand at composing works for the theater, and to stage them in palaces, the court, open-air theaters, processions, and in "corrales" or theaters in Lima and Mexico, the principal viceregal capitals. The staging of plays written in

America and Europe took place when celebrating religious feasts, important historic events, and the birthdays of kings, queens, viceroys, and bishops. In this manner the Spanish American theater developed and grew. Its complexities responded to the various traditions that marked it, the interests and concerns of its authors, and the particular colonial situation during which plays and dramas were written and staged.

Thanks to the early research by José Juan Arrom we have a panorama of colonial theatrical production. Recently, Grínor Rojo, Kathleen Shelley and Frederick Luciani have reviewed the drama of colonial Spanish America. A detailed history of colonial theater in Peru, including companies, artists, plays, and places of performances, was written by the historian Guillermo Lohmann Villena. Another historian, Rubén Vargas Ugarte, compiled and published pieces written in Spanish. The linguists Jesús Lara and Teodoro Meneses included plays written in Quechua in their collections of colonial theater. The recent book by César Itier confirms that the production and staging of plays in Quechua continued well into this century, and thus underscores the importance of studying dramas composed and represented in non-European languages.

Lately other researchers have discovered and studied the forgotten works of some Andean playwrights. This is the case of the investigations carried out by Severo Aparicio, Carlos Milla Batres and Concepción Reverte Bernal with regard to the theater of Francisco del Castillo, and Frederick Luciani about the *bailes* ["dances" or short pieces] by Juan del Valle Caviedes. Despite these efforts in analyzing individual authors and their works, to date there has been no comprehensive study that examines Andean theatrical works written in Spanish and Quechua within the parameters of the new multidisciplinary approach to the literature of the colonial period.

This book aims to fill this gap. It studies colonial theater by assessing four works written in Quechua and Spanish, some well known, others unexplored, in order to offer an evaluation that takes into account Andean cultural diversity. This study considers 1) the density of the different traditions embedded in these plays; 2) the complexity and variability of their messages in relation to their heterogeneous spectators, readers, and listeners; and 3) how the colonial subject reworks and often cancels the original models to show traits of cultural resistance or his/her concerns about the place of criollos, mestizos and Indians in the colonial order and the "republic of letters." But above all, the book, inspired by assertions of anthropologist James C. Scott regarding the "public" and "hidden" transcripts resulting from unbalanced power relationships, aims to decode the veiled messages resulting from the uniqueness of colonial situations as well as from the interplay of dissimilar traditions that commingle in the production and staging of these works.

The first chapter describes the peculiar nature of the encounter of Europeans and Indians and its impact on the development of theater. It underscores the common space—or "limitless library"—where the foreign and native cultures clash and interact in order to influence one another and, with time, change in an imperceptible or radical way. This chapter examines the links among the teaching of literacy, evangelization, and missionary theater as a means of conversion and also of submission of the native population to Spanish rule. The second chapter studies *Tragedia del fin de Atahualpa* [*Tragedy of Atahualpa's Death*], an anonymous Quechua work of the conquest cycle said to be written in the early part of the colonial period but more likely to be of the first half of the eighteenth century. The play and its continuous staging throughout the centuries situates it within the context of movements of rebellion and resistance in the Andes. This analysis enables us to understand the many meanings of this drama for the Andean public as well as to discern why this work is still relevant today.

The third chapter focuses on *Usca Paucar*, a little known religious work written in Quechua probably between 1690 and 1780, a period in which this native language flourished as a medium of literary expression. Addressed to a Native, mestizo, and criollo audience, the drama utilizes the classic theme of selling one's soul to the devil in exchange for material goods and the heart of a lover. However, when *Usca Paucar* is placed and studied within the context of the campaigns to convert the Native population, the paradox embodied by its theme of loyalty to God or to the devil is invalidated by a far more complex situation. The drama goes on to propose an alternative form of resistance for colonial Indian subjects such as the protagonist, Usca Paucar, a prince of Inca lineage turned pauper under Spanish rule.

Chapters 4 and 5 examine dramas written in Spanish. The former studies *Amar su propia muerte* [*To Love One's Own Death*] (c. 1645), a seventeenth-century religious play by Juan de Espinosa Medrano, a writer who lived and worked in Cuzco, and *La conquista del Perú* [*The Conquest of Peru*] (1748), a historic drama by Francisco del Castillo, a blind poet and playwright of the Mercedarian order in Lima. Our analysis of *Amar su propia muerte* attempts to show how the author transforms and expands familiar Peninsular themes thus transcending Baroque symbolism. Such variations send counter-cultural messages that could question the extant order and reaffirm the importance of those at the bottom of the social ladder. The last chapter analyzes *La conquista del Perú*. The revision of the conquest evident in this play, whose principal source is *Comentarios Reales* [*Royal Commentaries*] by Inca Garcilaso, shows the contradictory attitudes of the criollo elite. It also underscores the impact of Garcilaso's chronicle among groups on the periphery of colonial society—the descendants of Inca royalty, the criollos— that enjoyed certain privileges. If *Tragedia del fin de Atahualpa*, the first drama of the conquest cycle analyzed in chapter 2, is marked by messianic currents, *La conquista del Perú* suggests the debt of the conquistadors to the Inca kings, and perhaps points discreetly to the rewards owed to their descendants as well as to the criollo group that hoped to legitimize its ambitions by claiming Inca history and language. A *Conclusion* offers a summary of the principal ideas presented in the study.

I hope that the essays collected in this book will help to awaken critical interest in theater, the most influential genre of the colonial period. It is also my hope that the analyses of works in Quechua and Spanish, from the oral and the written traditions, influenced by Peninsular dramatic praxis and by Andean cultural currents, will help to reaffirm the significance of the unique traditions that throughout the centuries have frequently clashed but have also intertwined, thus shaping Spanish American literature and culture.

Hidden Messages

1
Movable Meanings: Evangelization, Literacy and Missionary Theater

INTRODUCTION

IN THIS CHAPTER I WOULD LIKE TO UNDERSCORE THE SPACE OF CULtural convergence where Europeans and Amerindians met, as well as the divergences that marked their complex dialogue in order to create a heterogeneous culture. I will call this place without limits the "library." From it the colonial subject offers his knowledge to conquistadors and missionaries and at the same time appropriates and modifies the principles of Iberian culture. Also in this limitless library conquistadors and missionaries are transformed by the urgency of the tasks at hand as well as by their contacts with American civilizations. Europe and America began to see and learn about one another in the controversial crossroads where the two civilizations met and clashed. In these intersections one can follow the move from a mainly oral and graphic culture to a print culture centered on the Latin alphabet, writing and books, and the power associated with the knowledge they represent. Central to this process is the evangelization and the teaching of literacy that takes place in two different directions. On the one hand, this exchange (evangelization and the teaching of literacy) marked the new and heterogeneous colonial subjects; on the other hand, these subjects reinscribed European knowledge within their cultural codes thus embracing divergent traditions. Later I will comment on how the lives of saints and religious dramas were reinscribed within Amerindian cultural paradigms in the staging of missionary theater, and how these representations sent messages that diverse spectators could interpret in contradictory ways.

Amerindian Productions

Traditionally, when we used to speak of the first contacts between Europeans and Americans we frequently thought of America and its inhabitants as a "tabula rasa" where Europe inscribed itself, thus quickly wiping out the contributions of the Amerindian cultures. Recent research has radically changed our ideas about the ancient civilizations of the Americas and has thus canceled our simplistic notions of the early contact period. Different disciplines have recognized the importance of Amerindian oral traditions as well as the centrality of the various modes of non-alphabetic "writing" (*quipus* [knotted cords], pictographies, paintings) peculiar to the ancient civilizations of the continent.

Specialists have underscored the importance of analyzing the exchanges among different sign systems and the diverse ways of preserving the past. In this regard scholars have begun to study the process of cross-cultural communication taking into account visual and oral sign systems of the Amerindians and their interaction with the Latin alphabet brought to America by the Europeans.

The Colonial Situation

With the introduction and imposition of the Latin alphabet as the leading system of communication, areas of knowledge (literature, religion, agriculture, medicine, cosmography) of the Amerindian peoples were codified or written down by missionaries and by bilingual and trilingual native informants. The first stage in the gathering of this information was its transmission to native informants in an Amerindian language. Then the informants codified or wrote it using the Latin alphabet, and frequently included images; the information was then translated into Spanish or Latin by missionaries and native informants.

European religious beliefs—Christianity—were translated into native languages. As was to be expected, there were frequent alterations and misinterpretations in this sequence of cross-cultural communication. In some instances the alterations were due to ignorance; in others, there were attempts to make the material more acceptable and meaningful to the recipients, or to reshape it in accordance with native cultural codes. In the early decades of colonization different sign systems often alternated with alphabetic writing.[1] However, writing finally displaced other systems, and some aspects of the other techniques were used only to underscore written points. The interaction of these different signs (oral, visual, alphabetic) as well as the ways in which they influenced one another, highlight the heterogeneous character of Spanish American culture since its early period. It is worth underscoring that this admixture was present before the arrival of the Europeans. In the Andean world, for example, the Inca empire or Tahuantinsuyu conquered and absorbed other ethnic groups. However, with the arrival of the conquistadors a new formula developed whereby Amerindian cultures are clustered and placed in opposition to Western culture.

This admixture points to a colonial situation in which Amerindian discursive productions are used, particularly in the process of Evangelization, in order to explain European rules and religion. Paradoxically, this desire to learn more about native cultures in order to evangelize and colonize, and, in turn, integrate the new subjects into the dominant culture, inaugurates a very peculiar process of acculturation. These exchanges are at the center of the dialogue between Europe and America because in the process the signs acquire multiple meanings according to the cultural universe of the receivers. Let me illustrate this with some examples.

In his desire to eradicate ancient religious beliefs, Diego de Landa (1524–79) imprisoned and tortured 4,000 Indians and burned many ancient Mayan manuscripts or codices in 1562. His actions provoked the anger of clerical and colonial authorities, and he was summoned to Spain. Landa later returned to America as Bishop of Yucatan (1573–79) and wrote *Relación de las cosas de Yucatán* [*An Account of the Things and Events from Yucatan*].[2] Thanks to Landa's history, the ancient rites of the Mayas that the author was so intent on destroying were preserved for posterity. At the same time, the descriptions of what some critics have called "pre-Columbian theater" came to us through soldiers, captains, and missionaries, who, in chronicles, histories and personal accounts, described the new things that they had seen and linked them to what they were familiar with. For example, in the Valley of Mexico, European accounts described the sophistication of certain performances. Hernán Cortés, in his third letter to Charles V, tells us about "[un lugar] como teatro que está en medio de ella . . . el cual tenían ellos para cuando hacían algunas fiestas y juegos, que los representadores dellos se ponían allí porque toda la gente del mercado y los que estaban en bajo y encima de los portales pudiesen ver lo que se hacía" ["[a place] like a theater, that is located in the middle of a square, . . . that they [the Aztecs] had for ceremonies and games . . . , their actors placed themselves there so those that were in the low and high places of the portals could see what they did"] (416–17). These and other references stress the Nahuas' interest in performing, and the visual arts. In the process of evangelization these preferences and abilities were duly noted and taken advantage of by the missionaries.

Teaching Literacy and the Gospel

After the encounter of Europe and America the different religious orders questioned themselves as to how they could best reach the Amerindian peoples. What methods could be employed in order to persuade the new subjects of the Spanish Crown to accept Catholicism? How could the missionaries go beyond linguistic barriers and superficial conversions to persuade the Amerindians to radically change their lives and beliefs? The answer to these questions was to initiate a campaign to instruct the native population through visual and other means. The essential components of the campaign were: 1) European missionaries began to learn native languages; 2) visual aids, including dramatic performances, were used extensively; 3) schools to further train the native population in the humanistic disciplines were created; and 4) European painters were brought to the New World to illustrate different aspects of Catholic dogma on canvases displayed in chapels and churches.

The Linguistic Encounter

As soon as the European missionaries began to learn the native languages, they produced catechisms and manuals of instruction to introduce Catholic dogma to the indigenous population. Some of these manuals were bilingual, others trilingual. Since there were no printing presses in America during the first decades of colonization, these books were written and printed in Spain. Even the catechisms written in America in Nahuatl, Quechua, or other native languages, had to be sent to Spain for printing and later returned to America for distribution. This appears to be the case with *Doctrina cristiana en lengua mexicana* [*Christian Doctrine in the Mexican Language*] by the Flemish born Franciscan Pedro de Gante (c. 1480–1572), printed in Antwerp in 1528.

With the arrival of the printing press in Mexico (1539), the production of catechisms and other books of religious instruction was accelerated. However, it is worth remembering that the production of these texts was always limited, as paper and ink were expensive commodities. Among the catechisms printed in Mexico, *Doctrina cristiana muy útil y necesaria* [*Christian Doctrine very Useful and Necessary*] (1578), attributed to the Franciscan friar Francisco de Pareja, is an interesting example. With its 36 illustrations, this bilingual catechism, reissued by the University of Salamanca in 1990, is typical of the manuals of religious instruction developed in the New World. Catholic dogma is offered in Spanish and Nahuatl. Its images help to reinforce preaching and to underscore the role of the Franciscan order in the evangelization of the native population. (See pp. 26, 27, and 28).

There are other interesting examples of religious literature (biblical legends, lives of saints) translated into native languages by Amerindians specially trained in humanities and Christian dogma. The legend of the life of Saint Amaro or Amalo is an example of cultural heterogeneity and shows how the new colonial subjects manipulated foreign ideas. In her study of this hagiography the anthropologist Louise M. Burkhart underscores how the original Spanish narrative was transformed. Native translators introduced in their version of the life of this and other saints

¶ Doctrina Christiana muy vtil, y necessaria, assi para los Españoles, como para los naturales, en lengua Mexicana y Castellana, Ordenada por mandado del Illustrissimo y Reuerendissimo Señor Don Pedro Moya de Contreras Arçobispo de Mexico, del consejo de su Magestad, y con su licencia impressa.

CON PRIVILEGIO
En Mexico En casa de Pedro Balli.
Esta tassada en dos Reales, y medio.

Title page of *Doctrina cristiana muy útil y necesaria* (1578), attributed to Francisco de Pareja. Courtesy of Ediciones de la Universidad de Salamanca.

DOCTRINA CHRISTIANA.

¶ Yniccentetl, ticmotlaçotiliz ynicel tentl Dios yca mo chimoyollo.
¶ Ynic vntetl: amo ticttapic rencuaz ynitocatzin Dios.
¶ Ynicetetl, yn domingo yuan ylhuitlipan, ateteayz çan tiquixcauiz intitlateomatiz.
¶ Ynicnauhtetl, tiquimmauiztiliz ymmota ymmouan.
¶ Ynicmacuiltetl, ayac mo macmiquiz.
¶ Ynicchiquacentetl, amota hauilnemiz.
¶ Ynicchicontetl, amo richtequiz.
¶ Ynicchicuetetl, amo titetentlapiquiz, amo tetech tictlamizyntlatlacolli.
¶ Ynicchicunauhtetl, amo tiqueleuiz ynteciuauh.
¶ Ynicmatlactetl, amotiqleuiz yntearca yntetlatqui.
¶ Yninmatlactetl reunauatili çan occa q̃ztica. Yniccentetl, ticmotlaçotiliz yn Dios yca muchi moyollo. Ynic vn cetl, tiquintlacotlaz immouã pouan, yniuhtimotlaçotla.
¶ P. Tlaxiquito yntenaua tiltzin sancta yglesia.

¶ Initenabuatil tzin tonantzin Sancta ygle-

en vano,

¶ El primero, amaras a Dios sobre todas las cosas.

¶ El segundo, no juraras su sancto nombre

¶ El tercero, Sanctificaras las fiestas.
¶ El quarto, honraras a tu padre y madre.
¶ El quinto, no mataras.
¶ El sexto no fornicaras.
¶ El septimo, no hurtaras.
¶ El octauo, no leuantaras falso testimonio.
¶ El noueno no desfearas la muger de tu proximo.
¶ El dezimo, no desfearas los bienes de tu proximo.

¶ Estos diez mandamientos se encierran en dos. Amaras a Dios, sobre todas las cosas. Y a tu proximo como a ti mesmo.

¶ P. Dezi los mandamientos de la sancta yglesia.

Los mandami-
entos de la sancta madre yglesia.

Teaching the Ten Commandments. *Doctrina cristiana muy útil y necesaria* (1578), attributed to Francisco de Pareja. Courtesy of Ediciones de la Universidad de Salamanca.

Detail of a Franciscan friar preaching the Gospel. *Doctrina cristiana muy útil y necesaria* (1578), attributed to Francisco de Pareja. Courtesy of Ediciones de la Universidad de Salamanca.

rhetorical devices as well as poetic imagery from Nahuatl oral tradition. In addition, they altered the narrative sequence and omitted facts that were important for Europeans but inconsequential for Nahuas (28). This researcher has reiterated how difficult it is to understand how a Nahua-speaker at the end of the sixteenth century might have interpreted these texts. The listener's or reader's assessment depended on factors such as his/her social standing, degree of assimilation of doctrinal material, and attitude toward the Spaniards (49).

It is also important to underscore, as Burkhart has explained, that even though the hagiographies were used as examples of saintly living in the teaching of neophytes, it is likely that the Nahuas and other Amerindian groups viewed the saints as totem figures through which the community could connect with divine beings (33). In other words, the material suffers alterations of many types; but, what is more important, its meaning changes substantially according to the cultural universe of the receivers. Burkhart remarks that in this type of doctrinal material, the process of resistance to the new ways becomes evident in subtle ways such as the selection of the material, the emphasis on certain events, and in the various ways in which passages of the legend are interpreted (51). Thus, in the limitless space of the "library," the Amerindian subjects adapted the Western doctrinal material to suit their own preferences. With time they created alternative versions to the material offered by the ecclesiastical establishment.[3]

THE SCHOOLS FOR NATIVES

The schools for natives were fundamental in the development of new cultural models. Instruction in Catholic dogma as well as the education of the native population were of paramount concern to the Spanish Crown, colonial administrators, and clerical authorities. Even though there was a special interest in the elementary education of the new colonial subjects, initially there was no agreement as to whether they should receive more advanced training in the humanistic disciplines (Gonzalbo Aizpuru, 111).

The more enlightened opinions prevailed, and in 1536 the Colegio de Santa Cruz de Tlatelolco, devoted to the education of sons of the native aristocracy, was established in Mexico. Its students were taught Latin, Logic and Philosophy, as was customary in the *colegios menores* in Spain. The sons of noble families were selected to receive this instruction because it was deemed that their acceptance of Christianity could serve as an example to be followed by noblemen and humble natives alike. In addition, colonial authorities urgently needed to create a group of middlemen that would help them impose Castilian rule on the native population. It was surmised that the newly converted sons of native lords could serve the Crown well in this capacity. Thus, language, as the linguist Antonio de Nebrija pointed out when presenting his *Gramática* to the Catholic Kings in 1492, and now religion, as taught by the missionaries, became the ideal partners of Spanish might in the American imperial venture.

Administered by the Franciscans, the Colegio de Santa Cruz de Tlatelolco represented the highest humanistic ideals in America—the perfect "library" for the intercultural dialogue.[4] Not surprisingly, the success of its teachers, as well as the ease with which its students learned Latin, Logic and Philosophy, frightened some of its patrons. After all, assisted by these disciplines the newly trained humanists might question the teachings of the Church, the principles of Western culture, and even colonial rule! On the other hand, economic pressures to use the indigenous population in other tasks (mining, agriculture, building trades), as well as the irregular support offered the school by powerful patrons and religious orders, made the life of Tlatelolco very uncertain, until it changed its mission and finally closed during the seventeenth century.

In this context, it is worth remembering that the objective of evangelization was to replace "the religion of the Devil" by Christianity. This is why since their arrival the missionaries were so anxious to find the quickest way to instruct the native population. However, we also have to keep in mind, as the anthropologist Jorge Klor de Alva has underscored, that the methodology used by the friars represents alternative ways of cultural penetration and appropriation—persuasion through the "law of the library."

That European letters and images are transformed and enriched in the limitless space of the "library" is a confirmation of the power of Native cultures to appropriate and transform the new ideas, and of their ability to insert their values and themselves in the complexities of colonial culture.

Evangelization through Visual Means

It was soon evident that the peculiar colonial situation required additional means by which to teach the Christian gospel to the native population. The missionaries recognized how hard it was to communicate through different cultural and linguistic codes. They also realized how fond the Natives were of visual representations and quickly perceived the ability of images to cross cultural and linguistic barriers. Thus, to complement the sermons and lessons in Christian dogma, the friars began to use large canvases with illustrations from the life of Jesus and of the key points of Catholic dogma (Gonzalbo Aizpuru, 32).

In the case of Mexico, as the young Nahua aristocrats were used to interpreting the pictographic "manuscripts," the association of images and letters helped them to learn Catholic teachings. For example, in the *Catecismo de la doctrina cristiana* (c. 1553) [*Catechism of Christian Doctrine*] by Pedro de Gante, illustrations in color represent the main parts of the Pater Noster, the Credo, and the Hail Mary. In these pictures life is represented by a tree, death by a mummy, and the Holy Spirit by a bird (Williams 1992, 6).[5]

The effective combination of letters and images made possible the creation of small books illustrated by the friars and their native disciples. These books were known as "catecismos testerianos" because the system of learning through images and its application to doctrinal teaching conceived by Pedro de Gante was made popular by the French Franciscan Jacobo de Testera.[6] Basically, the technique consisted of reworking Nahua glyphs into Christian symbolism. For example, to signify "I sinner, confess," a native appeared kneeling before a friar. Important components of the audio-visual campaign, as the Mexican scholar Angel María Garibay called it, were the confessions written with illustrations

(Williams 1992, 8), the creation of a phonetic system where the sounds of the Latin alphabet were associated with objects of similar pronunciation in Nahuatl, the distribution of small printed images or "estampas," and later, the creation and distribution in churches and monasteries of paintings and sculptures that would reinforce Catholic teachings.

Missionary Theater

In their zeal to convert the Indians, the religious orders used every means at their disposal to persuade the native population of the many blessings of the new religion and, of course, of the code of conduct that the acceptance of Christianity implied—obedience to God, the Church, and the Spanish monarchs. In order to convey this message, the missionaries took advantage of the attraction that the Amerindians felt for dramatic performances, for singing and dancing. The friars thus created "a missionary theater." For these performances some European religious plays were translated into Amerindian languages; others emphasizing biblical and hagiographic themes or Christian morality, were composed by Spanish missionaries with the help of Native informants, or entirely by Christianized and bilingual Nahua speakers.

Missionary theater was developed in North and South America. However, it prospered more in New Spain or Mexico than in any other region.[7] Perhaps this was due to the early arrival of religious orders and their commitment to converting the natives, particularly in the sixteenth century. For example, the "twelve" Franciscan friars that first created the framework for evangelization arrived in Mexico in 1524, three years after Cortés made his final entrance into the Aztec capital. The Dominicans arrived in 1526, the Agustinians in 1533, and the Jesuits in 1572. The orders favored the use of visual means including plays in the campaigns of religious instruction.

The objective of missionary theater was to instruct about Christianity, but also to teach the Native population the "virtues" of Western civilization so they in turn would become loyal servants of the Spanish Crown. The Indians were viewed within Aristotelian parameters. They, like women, were inferior beings, and thus had to be under the supervision of superior beings—for the indigenous population, the Europeans; for women, fathers, brothers, and husbands.

The testimonies of chroniclers and historians tell us that the theatrical performances were well attended. As there were many people, the plays were often presented in open chapels where mass was later said. According to the descriptions of these performances, they were characterized by the use of music, dances, and fireworks, particularly during the intermission and at the end. The plays were performed after the procession arrived at the missionary chapel or church and were followed by a Holy mass and mass baptisms. The actors were chosen from among the native population and were trained to recite the material in their own language. They had little time to master their roles and often improvised. As a result of these improvisations, there were non-canonical interpretations of Catholic dogma on stage. Songs and prayers in Latin added to the multicultural character of these performances.

The plays from a medieval repertoire were adapted to the American situation by underscoring native customs that could be useful in the Christian way of life. The translations were characterized by the use of repetitions. Frequently, live animals and plants were used to embellish the performances. Significant days of the Christian calendar (Epiphany, Christmas, Corpus Christi, festivities honoring saints) were selected for performances.

Due to the "civil wars" (1541–54) among the conquistadors in the Andean region, there are few testimonies of the initial efforts to instruct the native population through dramatic performances. However, some chronicles and histories confirm their existence and popularity. For example, in his *Comentarios Reales* [*Royal Commentaries*] (1st part 1609, 2nd part 1617) Garcilaso de la Vega Inca (1539–1616), the mestizo writer from Peru, describes the ability of native actors as well as the different themes of these religious plays. His depictions confirm the multicultural character of these presentations and stress their impact on European and Amerindian viewers. The former marveled at the intelligence and ability of the early Peruvians; the latter, remembering old dramas about their collective history, were attracted by the performance of religious plays with native actors and in their own language (1, bk. 2, ch. 28).

This well known passage from *Comentarios Reales* [*Royal Commentaries*] shows how the message offered by missionary theater could be destabilized and interpreted in contradictory ways by spectators of different cultural heritages. In this case the Europeans rejoiced at Andean dramatic ability and their quick assimilation of Christian dogma. For the Andeans, however, missionary theater reminded them of ancient representations. We know, for example, that the funerals of the Inca lords were enacted yearly in the *puru qaylla;* the *huaqaripuni* narrated heroic deeds of the Inca king to his subjects; and in the *wanka* it is likely that a woman accompanied by a drum recited the sovereign's singular accomplishments (Beyersdorff 1993, 218). In a previous passage Garcilaso also indicated who acted in the Inca performances and what their topics were: "Los representantes no eran viles, sino Incas y gente noble, hijos de curacas y los mismos curacas y capitanes, hasta maeses de campo, . . . cuyos argumentos [de las comedias] siempre eran de hechos militares, de triunfos y victorias, de las hazañas y grandezas de los Reyes passados y de otros heroicos varones" ["they were not lowly but Incas and nobles, sons of lords—and the lords themselves—and captains, and even field commanders . . . the themes [of the plays] always were of military accomplishments and triumphs, and victories, [or] about the heroic deeds and greatness of the ancient kings and other heroic men"] (1, bk. 2, ch. 27, 121).[8] Thus it can be argued easily that while some spectators—the Europeans—affirmed their religious faith and political hegemony through missionary theater, others—the Andeans—were sent back to a glorious past that the invaders attempted to cancel. Even more notable is Garcilaso's statement about how the skills of the actors changed the opinion of the Europeans that had viewed the Indians as dumb and primitive (1, bk. 2, ch. 28, 127). Not surprisingly, the author of *Comentarios Reales* [*Royal Commentaries*] praises the Andeans in a passage that is supposed to show the Jesuits' craft in staging missionary plays.

Thus, in the same manner that hagiographies translated into

Amerindian languages were marked by Native preferences that slowly eroded one or several aspects of the original message, it seems that among the Andean neophytes missionary theater helped to evoke the glories of the Inca empire, the past lost forever but preserved in memory. In the space of the "limitless library" brought about by the encounter, the new colonial subject enters into a dialogue with Western culture. The exchanges in the meeting place of the oral and the written, the image and the alphabet, of American and European knowledge, transform the speakers. As we shall see with regard to Andean drama, the new cultural products created in these crossroads of knowledge, will transcend the original prototype and their messages will have dissimilar meaning in accordance with the different universes into which they are inserted.

2
Historical and Cultural Contentions in *Tragedia del fin de Atahualpa*

Introduction

When we consider the conquest of Peru there come to mind the figures of Francisco Pizarro and his men who crossed the line toward richness and fame, and that of Atahualpa, the Inca king put to death by the Europeans. The confrontation and clash of opposing cultures in the Andes, symbolized by these historical figures, has produced an extensive body of literature of which the *Comentarios Reales* [*Royal Commentaries*] by Garcilaso de la Vega is the most acclaimed example. Similarly, the native historian Felipe Guaman Poma de Ayala in his *Primer nueva corónica y buen gobierno* [*First New Chronicle and Good Government*] (1615) offers one of the most striking iconographic representations of this encounter in his drawing of the meeting in Cajamarca of Atahualpa, the conquerors Pizarro and Almagro, the interpreter Felipillo and the Dominican friar Vicente de Valverde. These and other events that took place in 1532 and 1533 in the highlands of what is now Peru have been preserved in the collective memory of the Andeans and in many colonial and contemporary cultural manifestations.[1] The most notable are the plays about Atahualpa's imprisonment and death performed annually in cities and villages of Peru, Bolivia, Ecuador and the northwestern part of Argentina. As one might expect, each of these dramas interprets historical events differently, thus producing several versions of the meeting between Indians and Europeans and of the death of Atahualpa. One of the better known versions of this play is *Atau Wallpaj P'uchukakuyninpa Wankan* or *Tragedia del fin de Atahualpa*

The meeting of Pizarro, Almagro, Felipillo, Valverde, and Atahualpa in Cajamarca (Guaman Poma [1615] 2:386). Courtesy of the editors.

[*Tragedy of Atahualpa's Death*]. Written entirely in Quechua, it was performed in Chayanta (Bolivia) and published in 1957 by the Bolivian linguist and literary critic Jesús Lara.[2] These different versions illustrating how history has been reinterpreted and dramatized in diverse regions of the old Inca empire underscore the continuing opposition of the Andean people to the dominant culture and their longing for a more equitable social order.

In this chapter I will review key historic moments in the depiction of this struggle and point out how they can be related to the events dramatized in *Atau Wallpaj P'uchukakuyninpa Wankan* or *Tragedia del fin de Atahualpa* [*Tragedy of Atahualpa's Death*].[3] In order to appreciate the many meanings of the dramatization of this early moment, it is necessary to examine certain historical events that emphasize the claims and aspirations of the Andean people, thus shaping, as Nathan Wachtel and Franklin Pease have aptly indicated, a native interpretation of the conquest and colonization of Peru.[4] Let us survey some historical events to show how the people's hope, very frequently linked to the return of the lords of Tahuantinsuyu, has shaped their flow.[5] In fact, the return to the days of the Inca empire and the return of the Inca himself have acquired a particular meaning in colonial history making possible the contrast of the "old" order—Inca law—with colonial chaos. Not surprisingly this lack of order has been perceived as a "pachacuti" or world turned upside down by the Andean population.

The Case of Juan Santos Atahualpa

If we view the colonial period in Peru in reverse chronological order to show cases of native resistance, the eighteenth century provides two outstanding names, Juan Santos Atahualpa (1710?-1756?) and José Gabriel Condorcanqui Tupac Amaru II (1741–81).[6] The first spoke Quechua, studied Latin and Spanish with the Jesuits, and later learned "campa" and other dialects of the jungle. As a young man he traveled through Europe and Africa in the company of a priest. After returning to Peru, he claimed to be a descendant of Atahualpa,[7] staged a rebellion against Spanish rule, and gave himself the title of *Apu Inca* [Inca Lord] (1742). Even though there is no documentation of Santos Atahualpa's plan for reforms, it is known that he divided the world into three parts (Spain, Africa and America), claimed America for the Indians and mestizos (Stern, 43), favored the ordination of Indian priests, and encouraged his followers not to work for the missionaries. In addition, the new Inca announced that Englishmen would attack the coast of Peru from the sea to support his rebellion (Valcárcel 1946, 47–69).[8] Juan Santos Atahualpa's army was never defeated, due in part to its ability to withdraw into jungle territory (Tauro, 5:1930). There is also no documentation of the events surrounding Santos Atahualpa's death. However, oral tradition maintains that an envious chieftain wanted to prove to a follower of this rebel that this alleged descendant of the Inca kings was not immortal. To demonstrate his point, the envious *curaca* [Andean lord] shot and killed Santos Atahualpa (Valcárcel 1946, 68). In accordance with Inca traditions, his friends and allies preserved and revered his body for many years until it was later buried in a cemetery. Historians have indicated that the native population from the Huallaga, Ucayali and Perené valleys still remembers the deeds of this leader and hope for his return (Valcárcel 1946, 68–69).

The Rebellion of José Gabriel Condorcanqui

Better known is José Gabriel Condorcanqui Tupac Amaru II, a rebel leader also educated by the Jesuits in the Cuzco school of San Francisco de Borja for sons of caciques. Even though the historic context and the economic problems surrounding his rebellion are well known, it is worth remembering that he traveled to Lima in 1776 to ask that Indians under his jurisdiction be exempted from working in the mines of Potosí. He also claimed to be a descendant of the Incas and requested the vacant title of Marquis of Oropesa that had been granted in 1614 to a granddaughter of Sayri Tupac, the Inca from Vilcabamba who had capitulated to the Spaniards. The proud *curaca* [Andean lord] Condorcanqui was forced to wait in Tungasuca for the decision of the colonial authorities. Although his request was denied, he assumed the name of Tupac Amaru, the last Inca from Vilcabamba decapitated in Cuzco (1572), and began a rebellion that extended throughout the highlands. On 16 November 1780, this rebel decreed the freedom of the slaves. In this context, it is important to remember the early contacts between Tupac Amaru II and Miguel Montiel y Surco, a descendant of Inca royalty who had visited Spain, France and England. According to a witness to the judicial proceedings against the rebel leader, his former companion Montiel y Surco had at one time maintained that if the Indians themselves could not expel the Spaniards from Peru, it would be necessary to call on the English for assistance (Valcárcel 1977, 48).

The Literary Link: *Comentarios Reales*

Both rebellions bring to mind the *Comentarios Reales* [*Royal Commentaries*] of Garcilaso de la Vega Inca. It is important to emphasize that Tupac Amaru II, as well as other educated Indians and mestizos, read Garcilaso's idealized history of the Inca empire, probably in its 1722–23 edition (Durand, 208–10).[9] The "dangers" of reading the popular *Comentarios Reales* were later acknowledged when the Spanish administration reasserted its authority and ordered that all copies of Garcilaso's book be withdrawn so the Indians would not learn "muchas cosas perjudiciales" ["many harmful things"] (Miró Quesada, xlvi). The performance of plays about the history of the Inca kings and their empire, the use of ancient dress, and the wearing of the *maskapaicha* [royal emblem] were also forbidden (Rowe 1954, 29–30).[10]

In this regard, it is important to remember that the prologue of Gabriel de Cárdenas [Andrés González de Barcia (1673–1743)] to the 1722–23 edition of the *Comentarios Reales* [*Royal Commentaries*] mentions a book, *Nova typis transacta, navigatio, novi orbis, Indiae Occidentalis . . .* (Linz, 1621), written by Honorius Philoponus, pseudonym of Caspar Plautius, abbot of Seittenstetten (Austria).[11] In this work the author describes in Latin Atahualpa's supposed reception of Spanish sailors and soldiers sent by Columbus, and later of the discoverer himself. According to this fantastic interpretation of the discovery and conquest of Peru, Columbus visited Cuzco accompanied by friars[12] and soldiers. While in the capital of Tahuantinsuyu he was humiliated by the Inca king and later sent Pizarro to avenge him by conquering Atahualpa and his subjects. It appears that an illustration by the Andean chronicler Guaman Poma de Ayala lends credence to these fantastic ideas outlined in Philopono's book. Guaman Poma places Christopher Columbus, Francisco Pizarro, Diego de Almagro, Vasco Núñez de Balboa and Diego de Solís on the same ship (Gisbert 1980, 203).[13] Also one of the dramas of the Atahualpa cycle—the one performed in Oruro, Bolivia—draws together some of these fantastic elements including Columbus's and Pizarro's arrival together in the New World (Gisbert 1980, 204).

However, as Teresa Gisbert has indicated, even more revealing is the prophecy in Latin retold in González de Barcia's "Prólogo."[14] This prophecy contains the predictions commented on by Gualtero Raleg [Sir Walter Raleigh; 1544?-1618] in his *The discoverie of the large and beutiful empire of Guiana* (1596), and explains how the Inca empire will be restored by the English.[15] In this regard, it is important to remember that there is historical evidence of early contact between Andeans and Englishmen. It has been speculated, for example, that when Francis Drake (1504?-96) sailed the Pacific in the sixteenth century, he attempted to communicate with chieftains of this area and even offered rewards to those willing to revolt against Spain. In the same century, three thousand Indians rebelled in Potosí because they wanted to deliver that province to the English (Gisbert 1980, 204). Taking these facts into account, it is not arbitrary to propose that Juan Santos Atahualpa was familiar with some aspects of this background—perhaps learned while traveling in Europe or through reading González de Barcia's prologue to the eighteenth-century edition of the *Comentarios Reales* [*Royal Commentaries*]—and then proposed the English as potential allies in his fight against Spanish rule in Peru.

If a book inspired Tupac Amaru's rebellion and encouraged the descendants of the Incas to be proud of their culture, historical events and perhaps a prediction that mirrored old British interests help us to understand the alliance of Andeans and Englishmen

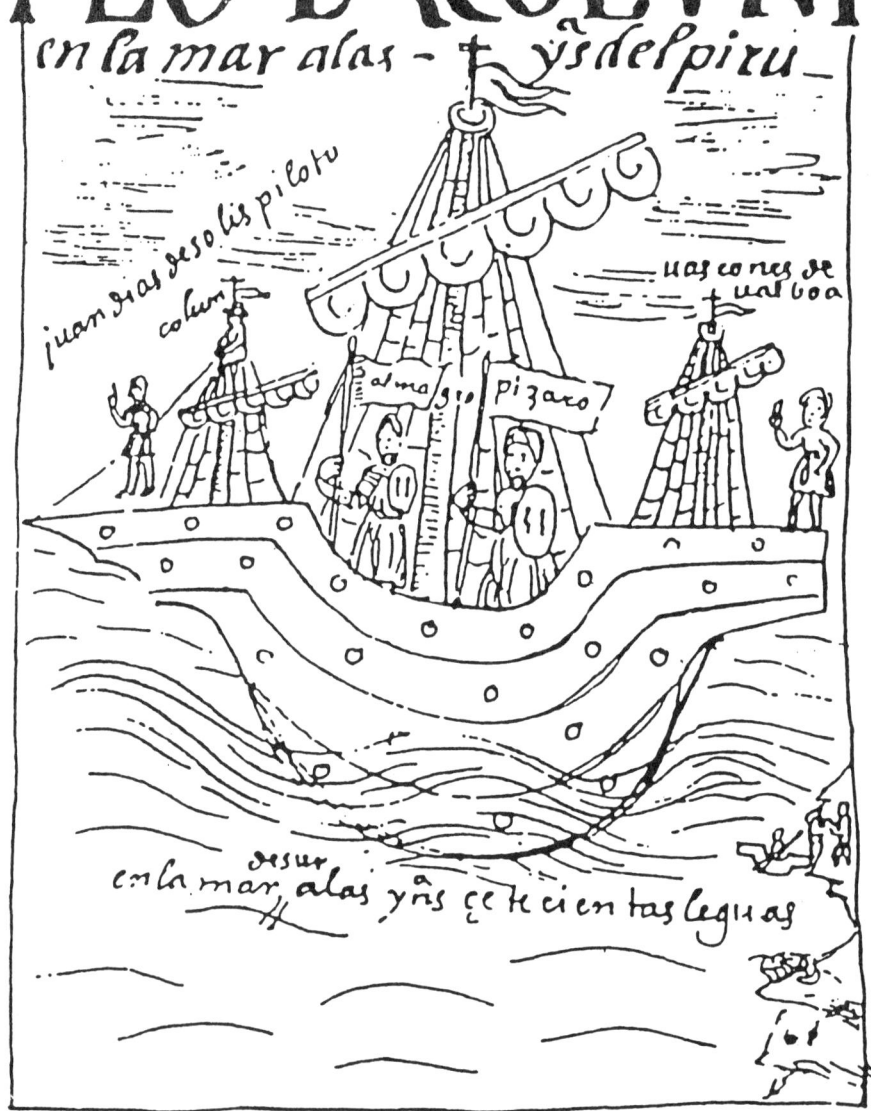

The ship of the "discovery" (Guaman Poma [1615] 1:46). Courtesy of the editors.

which Juan Santos Atahualpa desired and promoted. Both leaders, Tupac Amaru II and Santos Atahualpa, make claim to titles that apparently belong to them as direct descendants of Inca royalty. When they give themselves the title of Inca and promote the return to the old order, they allow for the reinterpretation of Andean history. This re-articulation brings us back to that initial moment in Cajamarca. In the same manner, the legendary death of Santos Atahualpa, the verified beheading of Tupac Amaru I, and the execution of the Inca king Atahualpa by the Spaniards, constitute landmarks in the development of the myth of Inkarrí, whose late origin has been suggested by Franklin Pease (1982, 57–71).

The Myth of Inkarrí

What is the myth of Inkarrí, or *Inca Rey* [Inca King], and how does it relate to the message of resistance and hope offered by Andean history and dramas such as *Atau Wallpaj P'uchukakuyninpa Wankan* or *Tragedia del fin de Atahualpa* [*Tragedy of Atahualpa's Death*]? José María Arguedas (1911–69), the Peruvian anthropologist and novelist, first took notice of this legend whose variants have been collected in different regions of contemporary Peru. The essential parts of this myth can be summarized as follows: Atahualpa Inca was beheaded in Cajamarca; however, his head was saved and buried near Cuzco. His body is reconstituting itself; once this reconstitution finishes, head and body will again be one (Arguedas and Roel, 34–79), and justice will be restored in the Andes. The "resurrected" Inca will reinstate the principle of order destroyed when the Spaniards arrived (Ossio, xxiii).

Underlying this myth is the fusion of the death of two Inca kings: Atahualpa, garroted in 1533, and Tupac Amaru I, beheaded in 1572 (López Baralt 1987, 26). In *Primer nueva corónica*, [*First New Chronicle*] Guaman Poma de Ayala draws the imprisonment and death of the latter in the main square of Cuzco and, as noted before in another drawing (see p. 44), depicts the "beheading" of Atahualpa.[16] Literary pieces hard to date with precision, such as the anonymous elegy on the death of the last

Tupac Amaru I carried in chains by Martín García de Loyola (Guaman Poma [1615] 2:451). Courtesy of the editors.

The "beheading" of Atahualpa (Guaman Poma [1615] 2:392). Courtesy of the editors.

The death of the last Inca king at the square of Cuzco (Guaman Poma [1615] 2:453). Courtesy of the editors.

Inca king, and ritual dances of the conquest currently performed in the Andean region, repeat this apocryphal version of Atahualpa's death. In the same fashion, a colonial painting, *Degollación de don Juan Atahualpa en Cajamarca* [*Beheading of don Juan Atahualpa in Cajamarca*][17] depicts the event through a reinterpretation of the death of the king that is almost identical to the literary statements. In the painting the beheaded Inca appears in the center of the canvas, while the priest Valverde is at his right, and the executioner at his left. These figures are surrounded by a rainbow against a black background dotted with white spots resembling hail (Gisbert 1980, 201). In this work of art the rainbow has been viewed as a metaphor for disjunction in which the head (Sun) has been separated from the body, symbolized by the earth and the Quechua people (López Baralt 1987, 62–63).[18] In addition, hail, shown in the painting as white dots against a dark sky, anticipates cosmic destruction in the Andean region (Guaman Poma, 1:57). It is worth noting that in the center, above the rainbow, are the conquistadors who judged Atahualpa shown in the form of a tribunal presided over by Francisco Pizarro. Above this pictorial space, there are four Incas representing the four geographical divisions of Tahuantinsuyu. Toward the left, the Inca throne is empty. The lower left portion of the canvas shows a meeting among Spaniards and Indians wherein the conquistadors point at and shoot the surprised Andeans. Even though it has been impossible to date this painting with precision, certain characteristics of the clothing indicate that it may be from the eighteenth century (Gisbert 1980, 202). Through these representations of the initial encounter of Atahualpa and Pizarro, it becomes apparent how history, literature and art, as well as reality, fantasy and myth, have come together to show how Andeans have decoded events and shaped a more meaningful version of history (Pease 1976, 130).

The Reappearance of the *Guacas*

It is essential to mention two very different movements of salvation and liberation that occurred during the sixteenth century:[19]

1) the rebellion of 1565 led by Titu Cusi Yupanqui, one of the last Incas from Vilcabamba; and 2) the *taqui onqoy* [dance sickness], a religious and political movement which portended a new era. It is important to underscore that in 1537, after his siege of Cuzco, Manco Inca took refuge in the mountains of Vilcabamba. There he established his court and from there he attacked the Spaniards. After his death, he was succeeded by his son Titu Cusi who organized an unsuccessful uprising against Spanish rule.

In 1565, the year of Titu Cusi's rebellion, the *taqui onqoy* movement gained many followers. Its messenger predicted the coming of another era in whose creation the *guacas* or local gods would participate and not the Inca gods. Juan Chocne, the prophet of this movement, promised good fortune to its followers. He also reinterpreted the conquest as follows: "el marqués Pizarro cuando entró en Cajamarca y venció a los indios [y] sujetó a este reino, había sido porque entonces Dios había vencido a las *guacas*, pero ahora todas habían resucitado para darle batalla y vencerlo" ["the marquis Pizarro when he entered Cajamarca and defeated the Indians and subjugated this realm, it was because then God had triumphed over the *guacas*, but now all had been resurrected to do battle against him and to conquer him"] (Millones 1984, 10). Using conceptualizations stemming from cyclical time, the founders of this movement predicted the end of the "Spanish era" and announced the beginning of another age, after the triumph of the *guacas*. Then the Christian god would no longer rule and the *guacas* would create and reign over a new and different world. In order to be accepted, all followers of this sect had to undergo purification rituals. The movement was deemed heretic by the colonial authorities, and its followers were persecuted by, among others, Cristóbal de Albornoz, known for his efforts at rooting out idol worship in the region. The devotees of *taqui onqoy* were punished in many ways: with beatings, shaved heads, fines, jail and exile (Wachtel, 289). As Wachtel has explained, the existence of this movement and its large following is yet another sign of disjunction which helps to confirm the split between Indian and European cultures in the Andes (288–89). It is equally important to underscore the role that native movements such as the *taqui onqoy* played in shaping what the German ethnologist W. Mulhmann has called the psychic infrastructure of nationalistic movements (in Burga, 112–13).

Tragedia del fin de Atahualpa

The rupture embodied by *taqui onqoy* and other such movements, as well as the decoding and reconstruction of history in Andean terms, mark the dramatic work *Tragedia del fin de Atahualpa* [*Tragedy of Atahualpa's Death*] and the plays and dances of this cycle now performed during religious and national holidays. Among the better known dramatic versions of this event, the Chayanta play has stood out because its discoverer, Jesús Lara, associated it with early representations described by Bartolomé Arzáns de Orsúa y Vela (1676–1736) in the *Historia de la Villa Imperial de Potosí* [*History of the Imperial City of Potosí*] (c. 1705). These early plays were staged in 1555, in Potosí, the South American silver capital, to pay homage to the patron saints of that city. Arzáns de Orsúa mentions eight dramas performed after two weeks of festivities and describes four representations which treated different events of Inca history.[20] They were performed for spectators familiar with the ancient and contemporary history of Tahuantinsuyu. In fact, the fourth drama described by Arzáns de Orsúa presents the ruin of the Inca empire with details of the arrival of the Spaniards in Peru and the imprisonment and death of Atahualpa. The author characterizes these works as follows: "Fueron estas comedias . . . muy especiales y famosas, no sólo por lo costoso de sus tramoyas, propiedad de trajes y novedad de historias, sino también por la elegancia del verso mixto del idioma castellano con el indiano" ["these plays were . . . very special and famous, not only because of the cost of staging them, their suitable costumes, and novelty of their stories, but also because of the elegance of their verse, a mixture of the Castilian and Indian languages"] (Arzáns de Orsúa, 1:98).

More recent studies, however, have disputed the link between the Chayanta manuscript and the play described in Arzáns' *Historia*. It has been pointed out that the Chayanta manuscript could well be a copy of this old drama, or that it might simply have been inspired by it (Meneses 1983, 523). The situation has become more complicated because, after Lara's death, his copy of the original text was lost (Meneses 1983, 524). Nevertheless, some critics characterize the Chayanta play as one of the earliest and richest of the Atahualpa cycle because of the development of the historic material and the prevalence of the Cuzco dialect of Quechua (Lara 1957, 32–33).

From a chronological point of view, the events described in this work take place between October 1532 and 29 July 1533, the approximate date of Atahualpa's death (Rostworowski, 176–77). The drama relates the arrival of the Spaniards, their initial contacts with the Andeans, and the death of Atahualpa. In the *Tragedia* the cast is divided into two groups: Indians (Incas) and Spaniards (*Auqasunk'akuna* or bearded enemies). Felipillo, the Cañari[21] interpreter, is included among the Spaniards. This initial division of the cast of characters corresponds to the two different worlds that will meet and clash on stage just as they did earlier in Cajamarca and will again in other historic instances. Even though the play is not divided into acts, it is possible to discern four important moments in its development: 1) the first is marked by dreams and premonitions announcing the arrival of the Europeans; 2) the second describes the initial contacts between Andeans and Europeans; 3) the third depicts the meeting of Pizarro and Atahualpa; 4) and the fourth stages the death of the Inca king and its consequences for the conqueror of Peru. Several key elements of the Andean tradition mark this drama, among them the following: 1) the configuration of the *pachacuti* or cosmic cataclysm caused here by the "beheading" of Atahualpa (separation of the head from the body); 2) the extermination of Pizarro and his descendants by fire. These paradigms remain on the surface of the theatrical discourse giving it a distinct meaning which refer us to cyclical time, to pluriculturalism, and to the future hoped for by the Andeans.

The Cosmic Cataclysm

In this drama Atahualpa's and Huaylla Huisa's dreams are basic to understanding the concept of the catastrophe unleashed by

2: HISTORICAL AND CULTURAL CONTENTIONS 51

the conquest. In fact, as of the beginning of the play the future appears framed by dreams filled with threatening omens. It is worth remembering that in the Andes, the deities communicated with people and made their will known to them through dreams. In Atahualpa's dreams, the Sun is hidden by dense smoke, while the sky and the mountains appear tinted in red (62–63; 70–71). Also, the red-bearded Europeans (74–75) appear clad in iron (64–65) and approach as if they were a red multitude (82–83). They are described as threatening characters because of their strange means of transportation, their weapons and physical appearance:

> tarukakuna jina
> kinsa ñauch'i wayracháyuj,
> chay chujchachankupipas
> yúraj jak'uwan t'akasqa,
> chay k'akichankupipas
> chhikacháchaj millma jina
> puka sunk' acháyuj,
> chay makichankupipas
> q'illaymanta warak' áyuj,
> chay warak' ánkuj ñaupinri
> rumita chuqananmanta
> nina raurajtan raphapan,
> chay chakichaykupipas
> q'illaymanta quyllurkuna
> illarispa tukukamun . . .
>
> (86–89)

> [They wear three pointed horns
> similar to the "tarukas" [deer]
> and they have their hair
> covered with white flour,
> on their jaws they all
> have red beards, similar
> to long tufts of wool,
> and they have in their hands
> amazing iron slings,
> their hidden power
> instead of throwing stones,
> belches forth flaming fire,
> and then on their feet
> they have strange iron stars
> which fade away in their glow . . .]

Adding to this gloomy atmosphere, the choir of *ñustas* [royal princesses] makes reference to a "Iman jáqay llaki phuyu" ["darkening cloud of pain"] and to a "pucayllujllan punkunchijpi" ["red torrent"], also signs of imminent disaster (82–85).

This incomplete picture that the Inca and his advisers see in their dreams and are incapable of understanding (68–71), brings us to a future fragmented by the death of the Inca and to the world turned upside down imposed by colonial rule. This metaphor is confirmed when the Europeans are described as having sprung from the innermost parts of the earth (70–71). In fact, as Franklin Pease has explained, after the European invasion, the world appears inverted to the Andeans, "mandando al subsuelo el cosmos ordenado que existía hasta entonces en la superficie, instaurando . . . una 'era de caos'" ["the orderly world that existed up to then on the surface of earth, had been sent underground, initiating . . . a 'period of chaos'"] (1976, 126). The laments of Calcuchima, one of Atahualpa's generals, because he and his followers will have to go to "úrquj sunqunman" ["inside of the mountain"] (158–59), or the rhetorical question of another general, "Inkallay, /jállp'aj sunqunmanchu/ yaykupuskayku ["perhaps we should take refuge / in the innermost parts of the earth"] (180–81), fit well into the redistribution of power and space imposed by colonial rule. In this regard, both the historic migration to the refuge of Vilcabamba,[22] distant from Cuzco, the sacred center of the Inca empire, and the play's dramatic proposal of taking refuge in the innermost parts of the earth could be understood as an exile from which the Andeans will return after the restoration of Inca order.

Chaos in the Andes

The chaos brought about by the arrival of the Europeans is depicted in the play with symbols of disjunction, the most notable of which is the death of Atahualpa. The first of these symbols can be observed when Huaylla Huisa and Almagro meet.[23] In this encounter Pizarro's comrade-in-arms only moves his lips, thus showing the lack of communication that the interpreter Felipillo attempts to mediate (94–95). This lack of comprehension will be verbalized later when Pizarro, in his meeting with Sayri Tupac, shouts through Felipillo: "Imata rimapayájtaj / jamuwanki purun runa, / manan watuyta atinichu / chay mana cháyay simiykita" ["What nonsense you come / to tell me, unfortunate savage? / It is impossible for me to understand your obscure language"] (128–29). To this Sayri Tupac replies: "Auqasunk'a puka runa, / manan ñuqapas watuyta / chay simiykita atinichu" ["Bearded enemy, red man, / neither can I understand / that language of yours"] (130–31). The second is evident when the lack of communication is repeated later in the meeting between Pizarro and Atahualpa, also mediated by Felipillo. In this encounter the conquistador only gesticulates and moves his lips (134–35). The third symbol of disjunction, now among the Spaniards, occurs when the Dominican priest Vicente Valverde reaffirms the evangelical side of the conquest, while Almagro contradicts him by underscoring its economic aspect (95–97). The fourth and most complex disjunctive sign is the interpretation of writing, where the lack of communication marks the cultural frontier between Europe and America. The Andeans associate paper with the *chala* (98–99), dry stems from corn plants, and compare writing to a swarm of ants, to llamas with their heads bent down, and to horns of deer (100–1). The paper—*chala* for the Indians—scratched and "painted" black with ink (106–7; 110–11), because of its color and the fear that it provokes in the Andeans, corresponds to the alterations of the solar cycle—the threatening black clouds described earlier in the play—, a signal that augurs a tragic event: the death of the Inca, king and god. Nevertheless, such a cataclysm articulates a message of salvation predicted earlier by Atahualpa himself: in the future his subjects will expel the foreigners from the Inca empire. The bellicose nature of this prophecy surely must have called the public's attention to the many rebellions against Spanish rule with which they were acquainted—those of Manco Inca (1536), Santos Atahualpa (1742), Tupac Amaru II (1780), and others throughout the colonial period.

As in other plays of this cycle,[24] here Atahualpa is also saved from fire by his conversion to Christianity. In fact, he is beheaded by the interpreter Felipillo (579), now playing the role of executioner. This change of roles is not surprising, particularly if one considers that in his *Comentarios Reales* [*Royal Commentaries*] Garcilaso attributes the defeat of the Incas to poor interpretation and not to the military superiority of the Spaniards. Seen in this light, the depiction of Felipillo in the drama is exact: he is the virtual executioner because his lack of linguistic ability has caused the ruin of the Inca empire and the death of its king described by him in the drama as a black savage (174–75). It is no wonder that in the cast of characters the interpreter-turned-executioner is listed among the Spaniards.

Atahualpa's death unleashes the cataclysm suggested since the beginning of the play by changes in the solar cycle and foreshadows the end of the Inca period: the storm breaks loose, the mountains crumble, water from the river turns red, the sky turns black, and the sun grows dark (178–81). In fact, even though the death of the Inca, king, god, and mediator, represents a triple disjunction—between Spaniards and Indians, between the king and his people, between the Sun and the Earth (Wachtel, 71)—the re-articulation of that death and the insistence with which Pizarro brings the head of the emperor of Tahuantinsuyu to Europe, will make possible the messianic hope later proposed by the myth of Inkarrí. Once Atahualpa's head and body are united, the world will turn once more and come back to the sacred time of the Inca (Pease 1976, 126) and the lost harmony will be restored (Wachtel, 71–72). Thus chronological history will be canceled by cyclical time and the collective hope embodied in the return of the Inca as depicted in *Tragedia del fin de Atahualpa* [*Tragedy of Atahualpa's Death*].

Poetic Justice

The drama takes us to still another dimension where poetic justice—the concept made prevalent by the Golden Age drama of Spain, that each character will be punished or rewarded according to his actions—projects itself into the present when pointing to Pizarro as the originator of the tragedy and punishing him with death, as foretold by the choir of *ñustas*.[25] Strangely enough, Spain, portrayed as an allegorical character symbolizing its monarch and also the Inca king, condemns the conquistador when he presents him with the head of Atahualpa and his royal emblem: "Imaynan chayta ruramunki, / Chay uya apamuwasqayki / ñúqaj úyay kikillá ntaj. / Jayk' ájtaj ñuqa kacharqayki / kay Inkata wañuchijta. / Kunanqa muchuchisqan kanki" ["Why have you gone to do that there? / That face that you have brought me / is the same as my face / When did I send you / to kill this Inca? / Now you will be killed"] (188–89).[26] In line with the concept of poetic justice and the predictions of the choir, the conqueror of Peru will die quickly: "Iyau, Pisarru wiraqucha, / qúrij, qúlqij aysasqan sunqu, / qan Inkaykuta wañuchinki, / llá kiy wañuytan wañunki" ["Oh, you, Pizarro, wiraqucha [godlike], greedy for silver and gold, / you killed our Inca, / you will die a tragic death!"] (186–87). But more significant in the dramatic structure of the play is the behavior of the allegorical character: Spain orders the body of the conqueror of Peru to be burned, together with his family and belongings (192–95). Here poetic justice takes an Andean turn and it is important to know why.

Among the Incas one of the most significant funeral rites was the mummification of the body. If the body was destroyed by fire, that person was gone forever.[27] The preservation of the body assured the everlasting presence of the dead person and the continuity of the cult that worshipped the ancestors' mummies. To eradicate this practice, the Spanish priests in their campaigns against idol worship looked for the *mallqui* or mummified bodies.[28] This is why Atahualpa in Andean oral tradition as well as in the dramatizations of his death is always saved from the fire.[29] The conclusion of the Chayanta play punishes the guilty Pizarro and restores the Inca to his correct role when Spain criticizes the conquistador while praising the king (190–93). In addition, it judges and condemns Pizarro according to autochthonous norms. This outcome in which poetic justice acquires an Andean turn serves two purposes: it exalts the values of the conquered people when the king of Spain, portrayed by an allegorical character, assumes these beliefs, and it brings out the messianic hope and the yearnings of the people so evident in several later dramatic versions of this historical event.

Seen in this manner, Atahualpa's death refers us again to two books mentioned previously, *Primer nueva corónica y buen gobierno* [*First New Chronicle and Good Government*] and *Comentarios Reales*, [*Royal Commentaries*] and to a historic event alluded to earlier—the beheading of Tupac Amaru I (1572), the last Inca from Vilcabamba, ordered by Viceroy Francisco de Toledo. In both chronicles, Philip II scorns the viceroy of Peru. These literary depictions add another twist to the symmetry that permits, on a discursive level, the exchange of the garroted Atahualpa for the beheaded Tupac Amaru I, and of Viceroy Toledo for the conquistador Pizarro. In fact, according to Garcilaso, in an interview between the colonial administrator and the Spanish king, Philip II scolded his viceroy and forced him to go home because "Su Majestad no le havía embiado al Perú para que matasse Reyes, sino que sirviesse a Reyes" ["His Majesty had not sent him to Peru to kill kings, but to serve kings"] (*Comentarios Reales*, pt. 2, bk. 8, ch. 20, 252). For the author, this and other criticism caused the fully deserved ruin and death of the once powerful viceroy. Guaman Poma also comments on Toledo's arrogance that led him to kill "a un rey y señor deste reyno" ["a king of this realm [Tupac Amaru I]"] without the consent of the Spanish emperor, the only one authorized to judge and sentence another sovereign (2:461). According to this chronicler, Philip II's rejection of Toledo precipitated his death. Guaman Poma also draws the former viceroy of Peru as a sad and humiliated person, duly punished for exceeding his authority.[30] (See p. 57).

Thus, in *Tragedia del fin de Atahualpa* [*Tragedy of Atahualpa's Death*] there is a confluence of the individual and the collective, the oral and the written, the message and the myth, so as to reinterpret the historic record and offer a new version of events. In this depiction the Andean past is evoked and exalted beyond the encounter at Cajamarca, projecting itself on to the present and summoning the future. This theatrical rendition of what happened centuries ago underscores the endurance of Andean culture and its ability to resist hegemonic values by redefining history in its own way. Seen in this light, the dramatization of these early events informs our understanding of the encounter of Andeans and Europeans while transferring it to a symbolic

Viceroy Toledo after his interview with Philip II of Spain (Guaman Poma [1615] 2:460). Courtesy of the editors.

dimension. In it, Atahualpa's death and Pizarro's punishment go beyond the violent rupture evident in their historic and literary representations and become paradigms of the justice owed, then and now, to the Andean people. In the following chapter we will see how a religious play also written in Quechua communicates a different understanding of evangelization for an Andean colonial subject, the prince Usca Paucar.

3
The Interface of Religious and Scenic Arts in the Quechua Play *Usca Paucar*

Introduction

IN A SHORT STORY BY THE CHILEAN WRITER ISABEL ALLENDE, ONE of the protagonists, a doctor practicing medicine in a remote hospital in Latin America, hopes to save his lover from death "even if it means making a pact with the Devil" (128). It should not be surprising that the doctor is willing to enter into a covenant with the Devil. This theme—making a pact with the Devil in exchange for health, love, or riches—has a long and distinguished history in Western letters. It appears repeatedly in Spanish literature, particularly in medieval legends. One of its most popular manifestations, dating back to Latin and early Romance versions, tells of the miracle of Teófilo, a humble steward who makes a pact with the Demon to regain his influence. Later, Gonzalo de Berceo (1195?-1265?), in the *Milagros de Nuestra Señora* [*Miracles of Our Lady*], compiled several versions of this account. In this repertoire Teófilo enters into a pact with the Devil only to be rescued through the Virgin Mary's intervention.

Interest in occultism and magic grew during the Baroque period of Spain's Golden Age and, with it, an attraction to the exotic and strange. Among the dramatic works of this period dealing with Satanic pacts are *El esclavo del demonio* [*The Slave of the Devil*], by Antonio Mira de Amescua (c. 1574–1644), a playwright of Lope de Vega's circle, and *El mágico prodigioso* [*The Prodigious Magician*], by the great Baroque master Calderón de la Barca (1600–81). It is worth recalling here that English playwright Christopher Marlowe (1564–93) used and adapted the German story of Doctor Faust (1587), translated into English in 1592 (Bowers, 123–24), to create one of the most memorable Elizabethan plays, *Doctor Faustus* (c. 1592–93).[1] Later, Goethe (1749–1832) recast various traditions, stories and legends around the same theme in his dramatic poem *Faust* (part 1, 1808; part 2, 1832).

The Devil Crosses Over

It is not surprising that such a popular and attractive motif crossed the Atlantic and became a major theme in at least two colonial plays written in Quechua in the viceroyalty of Peru. They are *El Pobre más rico* [*The Richest Poor Man*] (c. 1642), of unknown authorship,[2] and *Usca Paucar*, attributed to, among other authors, Vasco Jacinto de Contreras y Valverde (1605–67), a prominent cleric from Cuzco.[3] It has been suggested by Teodoro Meneses, a well regarded linguist and student of Quechua literature, that Contreras y Valverde most likely became familiar with Golden Age theater during his residency in Spain (Meneses 1983, 174–75). However, it is more likely that, since Peninsular literature traveled to America so quickly, Contreras y Valverde saw performances of the works of Golden Age masters in Lima or Cuzco. Meneses has also proposed that the cleric wrote the *Usca Paucar* in 1644 or 1645, years of great intellectual activity in Cuzco (1983, 174–75). However, after studying various linguistic characteristics of the Quechua used in *Usca Paucar*, Bruce Mannheim has concluded that it was written much later, probably between 1690 and 1780 (182).

Usca Paucar, auto sacramental del Patrocinio de Nuestra Señora María Santísima en Copacabana [*Usca Paucar, a Religious Play in Honor of Mary our Lady of Copacabana*] was first published in 1891 by E. W. Middendorf in a German translation based on a now lost codex (Meneses 1983, 167).[4] The Quechua/Spanish edition of *Usca Paucar* (1949–50) prepared by Teodoro Meneses,[5] based on the Sahuaraura codex (1838)[6] housed in Peru's National Library, is to date the most detailed and reliable. The plot of the play revolves around

Usca Paucar, a poor and embittered Inca prince, who, accompanied by his servant Quespillo, leaves his native Cuzco in search of better fortune during the early years of the colonial period. On the road the Devil or Yunca Nina, offers him great riches in exchange for his soul, a deal that the prince accepts by signing the pact in his own blood. Through the Devil's intervention, Usca Paucar wins the love of the devout princess Jori Tica and carries her off. Not long afterward, the Devil attempts to claim his slave and Usca Paucar, suspicious of Satan's intentions, flees. Quespillo and Jori Tica search for him, but finally it is the Holy Virgin whose standard is carried by an angel, who rescues the prince.

It is evident that this Peruvian drama shares two key elements with Spanish plays on this theme: 1) salvation through the Virgin's intervention, as seen in the "miracle" recounted by Gonzalo de Berceo; and 2) the pact with the Devil signed in blood, as in the previously mentioned works of Mira de Amescua and Calderón. In *Usca Paucar*, however, there are elements that did not appear in the Spanish works: 1) the protagonist sells his soul for money; and 2) a series of devotional scenes in which the protagonist, Quespillo, and Jori Tica allude to the cult of the Virgin Mary. It is then evident that in order to fully understand *Usca Paucar*, we must relate it to: 1) the interest of the new colonial society in material wealth; 2) the conversion of the Native population; and 3) Marian worship in the Viceroyalty of Peru. I propose that this complex interplay of influences—the literary tradition, the centrality of material wealth, the attempts to convert the Indians, and the Marian cult—shaped the characterization of the protagonist, his dramatic circumstances, and the resolution of the drama behind whose old theme of the demonic pact lies the dilemma of the colonial native subject.

Taking into account the diverse traditions evident in the play, I will first discuss the connection between religious preaching and pictorial art in colonial Peru. Through this discussion I hope to show how the two were reflected in missionary theater written in Quechua and addressed to the native population, and also how the messages of these religious plays could have been interpreted by the public at whom they were aimed.

Preaching, Painting and Acting

The messages of conversion and salvation were delivered from the pulpit and dramatized in open air theaters, convents, schools, and churches. They were written in catechisms and devotionals and portrayed in paintings, sculptures, and prints. Indeed, the spreading of Christianity in Peru was promoted by the efforts of the First (1552), Second (1567) and Third (1583) Councils of Lima, the arrival of different religious orders,[7] and the introduction of the printing press in Lima in 1583.

As I pointed out in chapter 1, in the years following the conquest, missionary theater was used as an important medium to overcome the linguistic barrier and to transmit the basic elements of the Catholic faith to the native population. Some dramatic works used elements of native Andean rituals[8] and others were translations of European religious works into native languages. Although, unfortunately, examples of these early efforts have not been preserved in Peru, chronicles and other accounts testify to their existence and popularity at the time of their composition. For example, as indicated in chapter 1, in his *Comentarios Reales* [*Royal Commentaries*] the Inca Garcilaso mentions the skill of indigenous actors as well as various religious themes treated in these early works.

Driven by the magnitude of the work of evangelization, missionaries from different orders acquired new linguistic skills and devoted themselves to composing catechisms and dictionaries to help in the Christianization of the Andeans. Under the influence of the Council of Trent (1545–63), the *Doctrina Cristiana y Catecismo para instrucción de indios, traducida en las dos lenguas generales destos Reynos, quichua y aymara* [*Christian Doctrine and Catechism for the Instruction of Indians, Translated into the Two Common Languages of These Kingdoms, Quechua and Aymara*] was printed in Lima in 1584. This was the first book published in the Viceroyalty of Peru and was, significantly, trilingual. The following year the *Tercero Catecismo y exposición de la doctrina cristiana por sermones* [*Third Catechism and Exposition of Christian Doctrine through Sermons*] was published. Beginning with the works of Domingo de Santo Tomás

(1499?-1570), who deciphered the structure of Quechua,[9] grammar books and dictionaries followed.[10]

These and other efforts at Christianizing the Indians multiplied as a consequence of the Counter-Reformation. As a result of this experience, the ecclesiastical authorities aspired to eradicate heresy in Europe and to convert the native population in America (López Baralt 1988, 171). In order to realize these goals, the Council of Trent issued a series of decrees advocating the use of visual methods to illustrate key aspects of Catholic dogma. By order of Philip II, the texts of these ordinances were read from the pulpit throughout his vast empire. In Lima, they were publicized in 1565 and 1566 (Vargas Ugarte 1951–54, 3:26–27). One stipulated that members of religious orders must give instruction in the "uso legítimo de las imágenes" ["legitimate use of images"], and also that "por medio de las historias de los misterios de nuestra redención, contenidas en pinturas y otras representaciones, la gente se instruya y se forme en los artículos de la fe . . ." ["by means of the stories of the mysteries of our redemption, contained in paintings and other representations, people shall be instructed and educated in the articles of faith . . ."] (in Tord 1989, 168). Period documents confirm the speed with which this policy was adopted in the Viceroyalty of Peru.[11]

From the beginning of evangelization in America, members of religious orders used images[12] that illustrated theological concepts too difficult to translate into native languages—for example, anthropomorphic representations of the Trinity. Several European painters arrived in Peru to help in the production of images and to decorate temples, schools, and convents. Among the most accomplished of these were the Italians Bernardo Bitti, Angelino Medoro, and Mateo Pérez de Alesio, who introduced mannerism into the region's art. Bitti was most influential because he worked and had disciples in Lima, Cuzco, Juli and Potosí (Gisbert 1986a, 23–24). Without a doubt, during the early part of the seventeenth century, Cuzco had already become an artistic center where European and Indian masters produced paintings, sculptures and other objects necessary for Catholic worship.[13] In addition to works of art especially conceived for religious services, books with engravings and individual engravings circulated (see Estabridis). Prints were also distributed to the illiterate population by priests eager to strengthen the evangelizing message (López Baralt 1988, 178).

The Marian Cult

Representative of this movement, where word and image converged to spread the mysteries of the faith, was Jerónimo Diego de Ocaña (c. 1570–1608). Sent to America (c. 1599) by the convent of Guadalupe in Extremadura to raise funds and to disseminate devotion to the Virgin Mary, this friar traveled throughout the Peruvian Viceroyalty and detailed his trip in an illustrated manuscript preserved today at the University of Oviedo.[14] To publicize the name of the Virgin of Guadalupe, the protectoress of his convent, Ocaña wrote the *Comedia de Nuestra Señora de Guadalupe y sus milagros* [*Comedy of Our Lady of Guadalupe and Her Miracles*] (1601), a dramatic piece performed in Chuquisaca [La Plata].[15]

Of equal importance for the spreading of the Marian cult were the images of the Virgin of Guadalupe that Ocaña painted in 1601 for churches in Potosí, Chuquisaca, and Lima. Painted on wood, the image at Chuquisaca was quickly covered by the worshipers with gold and silver plate and reproduced in engravings and in altars many times in viceregal Peru (Mesa and Gisbert 1977, 39). The literary and artistic work of Ocaña shows how both disciplines—literature and art—complemented one another and helped spread the religious message. They also illustrate the fruitful dialogue between these two art forms, the results of which are seen in several works of the period.

The cult of the Virgin Mary took a strong hold in the Andes because of Her appearance in Cuzco during the rebellion of Manco Inca (1536–37) against the conquistadors. Chroniclers and historians of the time wrote that the Inca's uprising was frustrated not only by the Europeans but presumably by divine intervention. The Spanish victory was attributed to three miracles—the church that did not catch fire, the appearance of the Apostle Santiago, and the intervention of the Virgin Mary—detailed and interpreted by Guaman Poma de Ayala (2:402–5) and the Inca

Manco Inca attempts to burn the church during his rebellion against Spanish rule (Guaman Poma [1615] 2:402). Courtesy of the editors.

The Apostle Saint James helping the conquistadors during the seige of Cuzco (Guaman Poma [1615] 2:406). Courtesy of the editors.

The appearance of the Virgin Mary during the siege of Cuzco (Guaman Poma [1615] 2:404). Courtesy of the editors.

Garcilaso de la Vega (*Comentarios Reales,* pt. 2, bk. 2, ch. 23–24). These two authors view and explain what happened within a religious context. According to Guaman Poma, the miracles are part of the divine plan for the spread of Christianity in Tahuantinsuyu, and thus the defeat of Manco Inca is not the result of superior Spanish weapons, but of heavenly intervention to safeguard the Andeans' physical and spiritual salvation (Adorno 1986, 18–27). Garcilaso offered a similar interpretation of these divine interventions. (See pp. 65, 66 and 67).

The representation of the Virgin Mary's intervention became particularly fixed in the collective memory of the Andean people and was transmitted orally and in writing by New- and Old-World historians. This in turn strengthened Marian devotion in the new viceroyalty (Vargas Ugarte 1947, 49–50). It captivated the indigenous imagination which saw in the Virgin a protective mother, as evidenced by the Quechua names used to invoke her (Garcilaso, *Comentarios Reales* pt. 2, bk. 2, ch. 25). Soon, in a syncretic process welcomed by the religious orders, Mary was associated with Mother Earth or the Inca Pachamama.[16] The veneration of Mary was reaffirmed officially when the Third Council of Lima (1583) marked the obligatory holy days in honor of the Virgin and introduced other practices to worship her (the Hail Mary prayer of the *Salve,* the brotherhoods of the Holy Rosary) (Vargas Ugarte 1947, 55).[17] The Marian cult and the devotion to the Rosary, introduced into Peru by the Dominicans (Vargas Ugarte 1947, 52–54), were rapidly disseminated as exemplified by devotional works in Quechua and Spanish and by two important shrines, Pomata and Copacabana, in the Lake Titicaca region (Gisbert 1980, 83).[18]

The Virgin of Copacabana corresponds to the Spanish veneration of the "Candelaria" [Virgin of the Candlemas] (Gisbert 1980, 82). Her shrine, like that of the Virgin of Pomata, is on the edge of Lake Titicaca and was cared for by the Augustinians (1588). The indigenous artist Francisco Tito Yupanqui used several images of the Virgin as models[19] for his sculpture of the Virgin of Copacabana placed in that sanctuary in 1614 (Ramos Gavilán, 116–17, 221). Surely the author of *Usca Paucar,* a religious work dedicated to this veneration, was familiar with some of these facts and, as we shall see, used them in the composition of the drama. (See pp. 69 and 70).

Our Lady of Copacabana as depicted by Francisco de Bejarano in the title page of *Santuario de Copacabana* (1641) by Fernando de Valverde. Courtesy of the John Carter Brown Library.

The Virgin of Pomata, 1675. Anonymous. Courtesy of the Brooklyn Museum of Art, New York (Museum Expedition 1941, Frank L. Babbott Fund, 41.1275.177).

3: THE INTERFACE OF RELIGIOUS AND SCENIC ARTS

Pious Postures and Religious Representations

In this context, and following the reasoning stated here, it is possible to associate some religious scenes of *Usca Paucar* with the pious attitudes seen in drawings by the chronicler Felipe Guaman Poma de Ayala.[20] I will comment on two of these from the play's last act. The first appears in scene thirteen, and begins with a brief description in Spanish[21] in which Jori Tica, holding a rosary, is kneeling, crying, and praying to the Virgin (III, xiii, p. 147). The second, the introduction of which is also written in Spanish, describes Quespillo and Usca Paucar kneeling before the Virgin (III, xv, p. 157). It is possible to relate both scenes to drawings in the *Primer nueva corónica y buen gobierno* [*First New Chronicle and Good Government*]. In one an indigenous couple, kneeling and holding a rosary, is praying before a painting of Christ on the cross. This picture includes representations of two spirals that correspond to the couple's prayers and thus indicate communication with the Christian God, a concept illustrated in the drama by the frequent prayers of Usca Paucar, Quespillo, and Jori Tica. The prayers will find their answer in the protagonist's salvation. Several scenes in *Usca Paucar* underscore the protagonist's devotion to the Virgin—even in dreams—(II, i, p. 67) and his belief in the power of the rosary to protect the helpless.[22]

In another illustration of Guaman Poma we again find an Indian holding a rosary and praying before an image of the Virgin. The last drawing reproduces an image of Nuestra Señora de la Peña de Francia-Virgin of Copacabana with the Christ child in her arms, both encircled by a rosary. Saint Peter is kneeling on the right holding the key which, in traditional iconography, opens the doors to Paradise for those who deserve it. We also see a scale on which the good and bad deeds of each person are symbolically weighed either to admit him/her to Heaven or condemn him/her to Hell. In his commentary, Guaman Poma counsels the readers to recite the rosary and other prayers to the Virgin, a recommendation that reflects the importance given by the Third Council of Lima and Pope Paul V to the Marian cult as well as the love of Andeans for Mary and their faith in the rosary. This idea is especially important in the devotion to the Virgin of Pomata with

Devout couple saying the rosary before an image of Christ on the cross (Guaman Poma [1615] 2:835). Courtesy of the editors.

An Indian saying the rosary before an image of the Virgin (Guaman Poma [1615] 2:847). Courtesy of the editors.

Virgin of Copacabana—Our Lady of the Peña de Francia surrounded by a rosary (Guaman Poma [1615] 2:841). Courtesy of the editors.

whom the Andeans identified because she was frequently regarded as the protectoress of Indian and black members of Christian "cofradías" or sodalities. (See pp. 72, 73, and 74).

Depicting the Angels

Just as popular as images of the Virgin Mary in the Viceroyalty of Peru were those of angels. These began to appear individually and in series and became a recurring theme in Andean pictorial art (Gisbert 1980, 86). In Europe the cult of the angels was accompanied by theological disputes, because only three—Michael, Gabriel and Raphael—are mentioned in the Bible, while others are mentioned in the apocryphal gospels (Bernales Ballesteros, 72). In 1516, the discovery in Palermo of an ancient fresco representing the seven archangels[23] and indicating their functions and attributes served to renew interest in them. At the same time, the Counter-Reformation popularized devotion to the Guardian Angel.[24] Teresa Gisbert has indicated that the pervasiveness of angels in colonial Peruvian painting is probably a result of the priests having substituted them for heavenly phenomena—stars, rain, comets, whirlwinds—, all Andean objects of worship with which angels appear associated in one of the apocryphal books (Gisbert 1980, 86–87).[25] Consequently, it should be recalled that one of the earliest representations of angels was in the Jesuit Church of Saint Peter in Lima. Their appearance in this church indicates, as Gisbert has observed, that the Jesuits had accepted the cult of angels (1986b, 59–60). The order confirmed the importance of this devotion when it made Saint Michael the patron of its Indian brotherhoods (Gisbert 1980, 87). Given the importance assigned to visual communication and theatrical representations by this order, it would be reasonable to propose that its members propagated the veneration of angels in sermons as well as in stage representations in order to make Catholic dogma more accessible to the Andean population and to facilitate their missionary work.

There are angels associated with the Marian devotion and also "military" angels (Gisbert 1986b, 60). The former are generally depicted in short skirts, with lace covering their knees, and draped with capes. The second, associated with the iconography of Saint Michael, also appear in women's clothing covered by breastplates and wearing helmets (Gisbert 1986b, 60–61). Art historians have indicated that the "military" angels are by far the most original in that they are dressed as nobles, carrying harquebuses, muskets, swords or lances. Each series also includes a standard-bearer, a trumpet player, and a drummer (Gisbert 1986b, 61).[26] Two important scenes at the beginning and end of *Usca Paucar* refer to the cult of angels. In the first, the devil tells about his defeat at the hands of the Archangel Michael, who caused great havoc in his ranks by burning the wings of some and by expelling others from heaven. The hand-to-hand combat between the Archangel Michael and the Devil described in the drama reproduces the essential details of this archangel's iconography, including the Quechua legend on his shield ["Who is like God"]:[27] (See pp. 77, 78, and 79).

> ñojan jhinapas sayani
> . . . .
> pulljanjayta uyapaspa
> champiyhuanraj huicapani.
> Chay erjjeri huarma huaman
> ñojaman cuttirimuspa,
> cuncaypiraj saruycuspa,
> ña qquirihuan, ñataj saman;
> jhinan jhuj chinlleyllapi
> chincachini samillayta,
> jhinatajmi Diosñillayta
> usuchini.
>
> (I, ii, pp. 49–50)

> [Yet I stood up
> . . . . . .
> and holding up my shield
> I threw my *champi* at him.
> That rascal, like a swift falcon,
> turning against me,
> stepping on my neck,
> wounded me, and returned with new breath;
> and so in a blink of an eye
> I lost my happiness,
> and even my God
> I lost . . .]

Archangel Saint Michael triumphs over Satan (late seventeenth century?), Church of San Juan Bautista, Huallabamba, Peru. Courtesy of Arzobispado del Cuzco (Peru), and World Monuments Funds (New York).

Military Archangel (late seventeenth century?), Parochial Church of Maras, Peru. Courtesy of Arzobispado del Cuzco (Peru), and World Monuments Funds (New York).

Standard-bearer Archangel (late seventeenth century?), Parochial Church of Maras, Peru. Courtesy of Arzobispado del Cuzco (Peru), and World Monuments Funds (New York).

In Archangel Michael's iconography, the devil is shown at his feet in a posture of defeat exactly as in the play. Usually the Archangel carries a palm of triumph in his left hand, and the divine power that helps him is represented in the form of a beam of light or a shining sword in his right hand. Although neither his clothing nor his arms are described in the play, the angel's warrior-like nature is highlighted by his fierceness in battle and the complete defeat of the enemy. Significantly, the figure of the devil, who fights with a *champi*—a mace covered with spikes used by Inca warriors—is indianized.

In the final scene of the play there is a procession of children carrying a standard with the Virgin's image. Usca Paucar and Quespillo, fleeing from Yunca Nina [the Devil] and his helpers, approach the image of the Virgin and seek her protection while the chorus recites a litany. The Holy Mother of God then commands the devil to return the contract signed in blood to the protagonist, while four demons flee before the arrival of an angel who, carrying the Virgin's standard, sings her praises and exhorts the faithful to follow her. The combat between the demons and Usca Paucar and his servant evokes the images, in paintings of the period, of standard-bearing military angels and angels devoted to the Virgin, who appear with a shield at their feet.[28]

It is likely that the motifs of the adoration of the Virgin, the worship of the Rosary, and the representation of the Archangel Michael were included in *Usca Paucar* to persuade the public of the kindness of these divine entities and their ability to protect those who accepted the Christian faith. The adoration of Mary corresponds to the Andean identification of her as the Mother of God and benefactress—as Guaman Poma and Garcilaso described her when they recorded Manco Inca's rebellion. The worship of the rosary, linked to the Virgin of Pomata, was introduced by the Dominicans and associated with the black and Indian sodalities also ruled by that order. Saint Michael was the protector of the Jesuit-sponsored Indian brotherhoods. These three devotions constituted symbols that were easily recognizable by the indigenous and mestizo groups to whom the works written in Quechua were mainly directed.

The combined and interrelated use of catechism, painting and drama serves to clarify and repeat the following message: the Virgin Mary is a generous protectoress and interceder; angels are effective defenders and invincible warriors; and those who accept the Christian Gospel and colonial rule will be protected by the Virgin, the angels, and the Spanish authorities. Conversely, those who do not will be destroyed as was the Devil in the play when his Andean *champi* was rendered useless against the archangel's power. If the drama is placed within this context, it is possible to discern the protagonist's dilemma and the many meanings of accepting the Christian Gospel in colonial Peru.

The Inca Prince and the Colonial Context

As we return to Usca Paucar, the protagonist of the play, let us remember that the drama begins with a dialogue between him and his servant. This conversation evokes the relationship between the noble but poor squire and his ingenious servant in the picaresque novel, *Lazarillo de Tormes* (1554). Just as in the anonymous Spanish narrative, the master in the Peruvian drama complains about his fate while his servant searches for food. The mention of provisions such as *chicha* [corn beer] and toasted maize (I, i, p. 25) reaffirms the work's Andean links, later elaborated upon by the dramatic speech of Usca Paucar, a prince of Inca lineage.

In telling his story, the protagonist contrasts the Incan past with the colonial present. When he recalls the former glory of his ancestors and compares it with his current situation, his heart fills with hate. Feeling displaced and forsaken, he finds no other solution but to destroy the detested present. His reference to the submissive servant's destiny and to how he is abandoned in old age (I, i, p. 31) is symbolic of his own situation and that of his people under colonial subjugation. In fact, the dramatic speech refers us to two historical circumstances: 1) the condition of the native population, forced into submission; and 2) the imposed monetary system in which Andean bartering and reciprocity were reduced to the same secondary position as were the Inca nobility represented by Usca Paucar and his relatives. In this new context the proud prince perceives misery as an unbearable evil, comparable to death itself (I, i, p. 33). This perception is reinforced when Quespillo, in a situation reminiscent of the squire-and-servant episode in *Lazarillo* previously pointed out, disguises himself as a beggar to get food, and even suggests that his master dress up in order to encourage a rich but ugly coca saleswoman to feed them (I, i, pp. 31–33).

The play's reference to the fire that destroys the Sunturhuasi ("Suntur-huasiyta ninapi, / ppuchucajta jahuarini" ["I saw my Sunturhuasi disappear beneath the fire"] (I, i, p. 29), a military fortress on the main square of Cuzco, which the protagonist saw reduced to ashes, turns out to be essential in understanding Usca Paucar's colonial circumstances. This allusion permits us to situate the drama's characters and deeds after 1536, during Peru's early colonial years. This was the year the Virgin reportedly appeared in Cuzco when Manco Inca and his army laid siege to that imperial city and were later defeated. (See p. 67). This historic event, which the protagonist Usca Paucar apparently witnessed, underscores the prince's disorientation when faced with the defeat of his own people and the overwhelming colonial circumstances that have changed his destiny.

Seen in this manner, the drama illustrates an inverted situation—"an upside-down world" from the Andean point of view—in which Usca Paucar has passed from prince to pauper. Due as much to this situation as to the values imposed by the colonial regime, the impoverished protagonist, like the conquistadors, has deified wealth.[29] Like them, Usca Paucar also transgresses and rejects the norms of the Christian faith, which he had presumably once accepted—he venerated Mary, attended mass, and wore a rosary around his neck (I, ii, p. 57). He does not hesitate to sin in order to establish himself in the new society, which, paradoxically, he wishes to destroy. In fact, when the Inca noble gives up worshiping the Virgin, casting away the rosary (I, ii, pp. 73–75) and entering into a pact with the Devil, he commits the sin of greed by abandoning Christian devotion for the love of material wealth promised by the Devil—the very wealth so central to colonial society. However, beyond the play's religious message, the protagonist's actions reveal an intention which was surely understood by the indigenous and mestizo public.

Usca Paucar sins because his home and lineage have been destroyed. Rejecting Christianity by embracing the Devil, he defies the new order in an act of religious and individual rebellion. Paradoxically, he risks being damned for deifying gold, the most coveted commodity in the colonial regime. Seen from this viewpoint, his salvation, like the oral and visual teachings of the Church, suggests the theme of the Virgin's mercy toward the Andean people. This is represented by Her forgiveness of Usca Paucar and the extolling of his faith, as well as the magnanimity of the Church, ready to welcome the repentant sinner. This reincorporation of the protagonist into the Christian scheme of things, cancels out his rebelliousness and integrates him into the Church and the colonial system.

Within this new order his condition as a colonial indigenous subject is characterized by the poverty and subservience which he rejected when he sealed the pact with the Devil. But, even more importantly, *Usca Paucar*'s dramatic plot emphasizes the significance of the message of religious salvation and colonial submission brought by the cross and imposed by the sword in the New World. The events described in this traditional piece acquire contradictory shades of meaning when we place them within the framework of the spiritual consequences of the conquest and colonization for Americans and Europeans. Thus seen, *Usca Paucar*, a nearly forgotten Quechua drama, is reinscribed in Spanish American literature, illuminating and enriching it by elaborating on an ancient theme and representing the painful reality of a different protagonist, an Andean Indian who struggles between sin and salvation, between rebellion and subordination. The next chapter will illustrate how Baroque symbols are reshaped by Andean tradition, the colonial situation, and the particular juncture of the female protagonist of *Amar su propia muerte* [*To Love One's Own Death*] by Juan de Espinosa Medrano.

4

Expanding Baroque Boundaries in *Amar su propia muerte* by Juan de Espinosa Medrano

INTRODUCTION

WHEN THE NAME OF JUAN DE ESPINOSA MEDRANO (1628?-88) IS mentioned in literary circles, his *Apologético en favor de D. Luis de Góngora, Príncipe de los poetas líricos de España* [*Apology in Defense of D. Luis de Góngora, Prince of Lyrical Poets in Spain*] (Lima, 1662) immediately comes to mind. This fervent defense of Góngora and Baroque esthetics was a response to an earlier attack launched many years before against the Spanish poet by the Portuguese writer Manuel de Faria y Souza (1590–1649). In the *Apologético*, a fundamental text of Spanish American literary criticism (Roggiano, 101–11), the Cuzcan author displays his knowledge of classical literature and affirms the creative power of poetic language. Espinosa Medrano's erudite defense of Góngora has been viewed as a plea for recognition on behalf of himself and of writers living and working on the periphery of the Spanish empire (Luis Loayza, 63–65).

Espinosa Medrano was also an acclaimed preacher, author of philosophical tracts, and writer of plays in Quechua and Spanish. As a playwright, he wrote in Spanish the drama *Amar su propia muerte* [*To Love One's Own Death*] (c. 1645), and in Quechua a religious play, *El hijo pródigo* [*The Prodigal Son*], and a mythological piece, *El rapto de Proserpina* [*The Abduction of Proserpina*].[1] He wrote most of his dramas while a young student in the Dominican seminary of San Antonio Abad in Cuzco (Meneses 1983, 12; Cisneros and Guibovich 1988, 337). Espinosa Medrano's sermons were collected and published posthumously in Valladolid by Antonio Cortéz de la Cruz, one of his disciples, in a book entitled *La novena maravilla* [*The Ninth Marvel*] (1695). *La lógica* [*Logic*], the first volume of a tract devoted to the philosophy of Saint Thomas, was published in Rome in 1688.

Espinosa Medrano, called El Lunarejo because of a mole or birthmark on his forehead, displayed in his writings the conception of culture—prevalent in the period—which was understood as an accumulation of facts.[2] He and others who wrote in Spanish America believed that through the assimilation and display of Western culture they could reach the Europeans and convince them of their worth as writers and intellectuals. El Lunarejo's life shows the fluctuations typical in the career of colonial writers, often viewed with suspicion or disdain by Spanish authorities and European intellectuals. Their talent and erudition appeared insufficient to remove possible "obstacles"—American birth, mixed blood, Indian origin—, standing in the way of their recognition. Let us now turn to some enigmas in El Lunarejo's biography.

El Lunarejo's Mysteries

Clorinda Matto de Turner (1852–1909), the famous *indigenista* writer, created a romanticized biography of Espinosa Medrano. In her study, she states that El Lunarejo is of Indian ancestry[3] and further contends that, on account of this, he was discriminated against by colonial and ecclesiastical authorities. However, Matto de Turner does not offer any documentary evidence to prove her assertions. Recent research by the literary critic Luis Jaime Cisneros and the historian Pedro Guibovich has allowed for a more accurate reconstruction of El Lunarejo's life. Despite their efforts, the exact place and year of Espinosa Medrano's birth as well as the names and background of his parents are still unknown. We do know that he was a student in the Dominican seminary of San Antonio Abad in Cuzco, and that in 1654 he graduated from the Jesuit university of San Ignacio de Loyola. In the years that followed he gained recognition as a preacher and writer. The *Apologético* was published in Lima in 1662 and in 1664 the *Panegírica declamación por la protección de las ciencias y estudios* [*Panegyric Declamation for the Protection of Sciences and other Studies*] and the *Discurso* [*Discourse*]⁴ defending the right to be appointed to ecclesiastical posts of those who participated in the competition for such posts vis-a-vis those who were recommended by others, also appeared in Lima.

Statements made by El Lunarejo in the first edition of the *Apologético*,⁵ show his identification with the New World as well as his love for his native land and its inhabitants (Núñez Cáceres 1989, 72–75).⁶ In this regard it is important to underscore that in the segment dedicated to the reader ["Al lector"] the author comments: "pero ¿qué puede haber bueno en las Indias? ¿Qué puede haber que contente a los europeos, que desta suerte dudan? Sátiros nos juzgan, tritones nos presumen, que, brutos de alma, en vano se alientan a desmentirnos máscaras de la humanidad" ["But, what good things do the Indies have? What could satisfy the Europeans that doubt that anything good could come from the Indies? They think we are satyrs; they presume we are tritons, with the facade of humans trying to disguise our animal-like nature"] (41).⁷ It is worth noting that Covarrubias in his *Tesoro de la lengua castellana* [*Treasure of the Spanish Language*] (1611), equates satyrs with monsters, and goes on to quote Pliny's description of these creatures: "animales quadrúpedos, que se crían en los montes subsolanos de las Indias [Orientales], los quales tienen rostros de hombres y corren en dos pies" ["four legged animals that inhabit the sunny mountains of the [Eastern] Indies; they have human faces and run on two feet"]. El Lunarejo aims to contradict these erroneous judgments while praising the intellectual gifts of writers from his native Peru through the erudition of the *Apologético* and other works.

Based on comments made by his contemporaries and by himself, we do know that the author's talents were not quickly recognized. The available documentation mentions "exclusiones" ["exclusions"] experienced by the author. For example, in the preliminary pages of the *Discurso,* the Augustinian friar Francisco de Loyola y Vergara underscores El Lunarejo's talent and expresses his astonishment at the negligible recognition the author has received. In the same document, Espinosa Medrano also complains about being forgotten (*Discurso,* in Cisneros and Guibovich 1989, 106). Considering the repetition of these and similar remarks, one cannot help but wonder if the author had earlier sought an ecclesiastical post without success; or if, as asserted by Cisneros and Guibovich, he wrote and published the *Discurso* to prove his case of past injustices (1989, 104). These possibilities bring to mind several questions. Why was such a talented person passed over? Why was Espinosa Medrano criticized even after his death?[8] Even though the available documentation does not allow for a definitive response, we do know that Espinosa Medrano was not appointed as a parish priest in Chincheros until 1668 and had to wait nine years (1677) to be appointed parish priest in San Cristóbal, an ecclesiastical jurisdiction in Cuzco with many Indian members. In 1682 El Lunarejo occupied the post of "Canónigo magistral" in the Cathedral of Cuzco (Cisneros and Guibovich 1988, 339–41); and four years later, in 1686, he became "Chantre de la Catedral" in Cuzco. Despite these appointments, criticism persisted even after his death.

The recent finding by Pedro Guibovich of a copy of Espinosa Medrano's last will and testament in the Archives of the Archbishopric of Lima does not reveal any information about his family or birth. This lack of data would tend to confirm his illegitimate birth insinuated in the "Prólogo" of *La novena maravilla* [*The Ninth Marvel*]. There the writer is labeled "hijo de sus obras" ["son of his works"]. It is worth noting that the inventory of his possessions confirms that, at the time of his death, El Lunarejo enjoyed a respectable economic position (Guibovich 1992, 1–31).[9]

Culture, Power and Religion

Perhaps Espinosa Medrano's unstable relationship with ecclesiastical authorities, together with his contacts with Dominicans and Jesuits, contributed to his acute awareness of being a colonial subject. In fact, in the "Prefacio del autor" ["Preface by the Author"] to *La lógica* he responds to European contentions that viewed "los estudios de los hombres del Nuevo Mundo . . . [como] bárbaros" ["the studies by the men from the New World as barbaric"] (325). He further characterized his native land as "un lugar aventajado de la tierra, donde sonríe un cielo mejor" ["a privileged place on earth, where a better sky smiles"]; this sky shelters "grandes hombres . . . en letras, en ingenio, en doctrina, en amenidad de costumbres y en santidad" ["great men in letters, in talent, in learning, in elegance of manners and in sanctity"] (326–27). Thus, with these words Espinosa Medrano attempts to vindicate Peru and its intelligentsia. In so doing, he reaffirms his own worth and that of his peers, as well as their ability and right to assimilate European culture and produce works comparable to those of famous Old World authors.

This affirmation of the ability of Peruvian intellectuals goes hand in hand with his search for the means of disseminating European knowledge. That is to say, Espinosa Medrano and others like him believed that Western culture had a fundamental role to play in the Andes. When discussing the *Apologético*, Mario Vargas Llosa movingly explained the efforts made by El Lunarejo in his writings: "en su texto, erudito, belicoso, atiborrado de pasión y de metáforas, hay una voluntad de apropiación de una cultura que adelanta lo que es hoy, intelectualmente, América Latina" ["in his erudite and feisty texts, replete with passion and metaphors, there is a will to appropriate [European] culture that foregrounds, intellectually, what Latin America is today"] (895). In El Lunarejo the will to appropriate goes beyond the *Apologético* and imprints all his writings.

It is important to underscore immediately that Espinosa Medrano's attitude is not unique.[10] The historian Raúl Porras Barrenechea has pointed out that in seventeenth-century Peru clergymen continued their efforts to master Native languages. Also during this period literary models from Spain, particularly in poetry, were adapted to the Quechua language and new artistic forms were developed. Porras Barrenechea further asserts that these efforts to integrate Western and Andean literary cultures were evident in church sermons as well as in poems and dramas written in the language of the Incas (xvi). All of this shows, particularly in Cuzco, the emergence of a pluricultural society where Quechua and Aymara were spoken and considered to be on an equal basis with Spanish. Thus, it can be assumed that at least an elite audience, well versed in Quechua and Spanish, was able to understand difficult metaphors and even to decode hidden messages presented in sermons, poems, and plays.[11] Some of these listeners were descendants of Inca royalty, first linked to conquistadors and later to members of the colonial bureaucracy. Others were *curacas* [Andean lords] and their relatives and children, mestizos interested in pursuing an ecclesiastical career,[12] and Indians that worked as interpreters. Priests and local functionaries well versed in the *runa simi* [Quechua] made up a third group of readers, spectators, and listeners.

It is important to recall that when Francisco de Borja y Aragón, Príncipe de Esquilache, was Viceroy of Peru (1615–21), he attempted to organize the education of the native elite. He was particularly interested in the sons of caciques whose work as intermediaries was essential for the exploitation of Andean agriculture and metallurgy (Millones 1987, 160). With this objective, Viceroy Esquilache established two schools for the Indian elite, San Francisco de Borja in Cuzco (1619)[13] and the Príncipe in Lima (1620). Both were administered by the Jesuits, who taught writing, reading, religion, and Latin.[14] In Cuzco, the ancient capital of the Incas, there were two schools devoted to secondary education, San Bernardo (1619), administered by the Jesuits,[15] and San Antonio Abad administered by the Dominicans (1598), where El Lunarejo studied and taught.[16]

Espinosa Medrano's connection to Dominicans and Jesuits, the two religious orders that controlled education in Cuzco,[17] is significant. He was educated in San Antonio Abad, a Dominican seminary and secondary school, and later graduated from the Jesuit university of Saint Ignatius of Loyola. It is well known that both orders were at the forefront of the defense of the rights of the Native population. Furthermore, the followers of Saint Ignatius of Loyola were interested in creating a Catholic theocracy in Peru taking advantage of Inca governmental structures as well as of Inca royalty (Duviols, 229).[18] It is also important to underscore that in Jesuit schools the students were instructed in declamation and scenic arts through the composition of short pieces known as "decurias."[19] To develop their rhetorical skills, the students composed longer plays performed during private and public celebrations (Martín, 43–48).[20] Even though the staging of plays and interludes was later forbidden in the cloisters of the Compañía, the "decurias" continued to be presented to a smaller and privileged audience (Vargas Ugarte 1943, xxxiv–v).[21] In fact, aside from the "corrales" or open-air theaters,[22] cloisters and schools were the preferred spaces where religious plays, interludes and dramas were performed.

Amar su propia muerte,[23] a Youthful Drama

Taking into account colonial theatrical fashion, it may be safely assumed that Espinosa Medrano's *Amar su propia muerte* [*To Love One's Own Death*], was written and performed while the author was a student at San Antonio Abad (Vargas Ugarte 1943, xxx),[24] probably around 1645. This important drama was discovered by Rubén Vargas Ugarte in the National Library of Peru in an unpaginated volume of miscellany and remained unpublished until 1932.[25] Unfortunately, its only known manuscript was destroyed in a fire (1943) at the National Library of Peru that severely damaged its collections.

Considering *Amar*'s Baroque twists, treatment of honor, use of different meters, and the biblical theme of its plot, one may assume, as did Vargas Ugarte, that El Lunarejo was familiar with the works of the masters of Spanish Golden Age theater, Lope de Vega, Calderón de la Barca and Tirso de Molina (1943, xxx). This is not surprising, since Irving A. Leonard in his *Books of the Brave* explained how quickly works published in Spain reached the American capitals. In fact, the plot of *Amar* is based, as was frequently the case in Golden Age drama, on an episode from the Old Testament (Judges 4:1–24). It narrates the defeat of Sísara, a Canaanite general, by Barac, commander of the Israeli armies, and the fulfillment of a prophecy, "The glory of this campaign will not be for you [Barac], because the Lord will deliver Sisera unto the hands of a woman" (Judges 4:9). In the Bible as in the drama, Sísara is assassinated by Jael, the wife of Heber Cineo; the plot becomes complicated because the couple (Jael and Heber Cineo) lived under the protection of Jabín, the Canaanite king.

Following theatrical practices of the period, Espinosa Medrano transforms the biblical story into a play of honor, complete with a *gracioso* and a love triangle now increased to four as three men (the Canaanite general Sísara, his king Jabín, and Heber Cineo, the husband) are in love with Jael, and situates it in a remote land and time. A first reading of this drama will tend to classify it as a colonial imitation of Golden Age theater. It is my contention, however, that the play subverts its Peninsular models and uses the biblical narration to bring to the fore situations that can be meaningful in colonial Peru. An analysis of the following cultural categories will lead us to a different reading of the play: 1) references to the colonial world; 2) dreams, premonitions, and natural phenomena; 3) and the role of two women, Jael and Débora, in the development of the action. This examination will expose the hybrid[26] nature of the play and will also reveal how the ambivalence of Baroque discourse can be manipulated to question the colonial order.

THE VICEREGAL WORLD

In the drama there are only two references to Peruvian colonial society. The first appears when Bato and Mosco, two servants, crack open a large earthen jar in which the *gracioso* Vigote is hidden. As it is very heavy, Bato remarks: "Parece que tiene azogue, / que la meneo yo apenas" ["It seems to be filled with quicksilver, / I can barely move it"]. In an aside, Vigote refers to his trembling out of fear of being discovered: "Si hubiera dicho azogado / no errara" ["If he had said trembling ["azogado"] / he would not have erred"] (II, xi, p. 269). These comments must be viewed in the following context. At the end of the sixteenth century rich mines of quicksilver were discovered in Huancavelica, a city near Cuzco. The extraction of this mineral was first accomplished through the open pit system, and later by digging tunnels. As ventilation was insufficient, the *mitayos* [Indian conscripted laborers] breathed in the quicksilver dust and, as a consequence, began to tremble and died shortly afterwards. The discreet reference to this illness to characterize Vigote's trembling with fear, surely brought to the minds of the spectators the deadly work that the Indians were required to perform in Huancavelica and in the nearby silver mines of Potosí.

The second reference to colonial society also appears in a comic context. The servant Bato makes fun of Mosco because he has milked a he-goat ["cabrón"]. Mosco answers, "Mentís, no fue sino cabra" ["You are lying; it was a nanny goat"]; and Bato responds, "Con más barba que un oidor" ["With a longer beard than a judge"] (III, xii, pp. 312–13). It is well known that the he-goat has traditionally been associated with lewdness. Covarrubias in his *Tesoro* indicates that because in antiquity this animal destroyed the vineyards, it was sacrificed to Bacchus, the god of wine; later the he-goat was associated with the devil and complaisant husbands (256–57). When linking the he-goat mistakenly milked by Mosco to colonial jurists, Espinosa Medrano followed Baroque practices that criticized the prevalent social order through puns and plays on words.[27] Thus, indirectly, the jurist is linked to drunkenness, demonic rites, lewdness, and the disgrace of cuckold husbands. Using the stage, El Lunarejo brings to the fore problems of the mining industry and the exploitation of the Indian population as well as the vices frequently associated with corrupt and powerful members of the judicial elite. The heterogeneous theater-going public that attended the performances of colonial plays, dramas, and interludes surely was able to understand the hidden meaning offered by the author's play on words.

Dreams, Premonitions and Natural Phenomena

The close analysis of *Amar* shows how the Andean world penetrates Baroque symbols to produce an unstable cultural product since its message could be construed in different ways by the mixed public attending the performance. Let us now turn to a key episode of the play to see how this instability functions. The impending defeat of the Canaanites by the Israelites is announced by dreams, premonitions, heavenly signs, and catastrophes. For example, King Jabín dreams that he is killed by his friend and ally, Heber Cineo (II, iii, p. 278). Dreams were of paramount importance in the Andean world because they were considered supernatural experiences through which divine beings communicated with believers in order to advise, warn or berate them (Rowe 1963, 293; Millones 130). In this case, the dreams forewarn the king of his friend's murderous intentions.

The many heavenly omens present in the drama frighten Sísara and his army, and convince King Jabín that heaven is against them (II, iv, p. 279). His premonitory dreams as well as the celestial signs can be interpreted as an allusion to one of the symbolic divisions of space[28] in the Andean world: the *Hanan Pacha* or place in which the deities reside; the *Cay Pacha* or place in the middle where humans and animals live; and the *Ucu Pacha*, or underworld (Pease 1982, 27–28) inhabited by negative forces and transgressors (Rowe 1963, 298).[29] In the drama this division of space is reinforced through the personification of heaven by action verbs such as "pelea" [fight] and "baja" [come down] (II, v, p. 283). Another important sign, the appearance of a comet (II, v, pp. 281–82), again presents the struggle of celestial divinities against Sísara and his people.[30] In this regard, it is worth remembering that comets were so important in the Andean world that they were named according to their characteristics. Unfailingly, they announced major catastrophes.[31] The Andean historical record shows that comets and lightening forewarned the Incas of the death of their sovereign Huayna Capac before the arrival of the Spaniards, of the struggle between his sons and heirs, Atahualpa and Huascar, and of the final destruction of the empire (Garcilaso, *Comentarios Reales* [*Royal Commentaries*] pt. 2, bk. 9, 249). In *Amar* the comet predicts two tragic events: King Jabín's defeat and the death of General Sísara. The end of Canaanite rule, however, is portended by an earthquake (III, i, pp. 292–93). It is known that in the Andean world an earthquake is associated with the *pachacuti*, a cataclysm that augurs the end of a cycle and the creation of a new age. Thus, it can be assumed that in the drama the earthquake announces the end of Canaanite rule and the beginning of Israelite rule. In this manner the play mixes Western chronological development of events with references that easily can be associated with Andean cyclical time.

But, how does the author picture Canaanite rule whose end is quickly approaching? To answer this question one must look at how Espinosa Medrano characterizes the Canaanite elite. General Sísara's arrogance is evident when he dares to challenge the heavenly warnings (II, v, p. 282); King Jabín forgets his responsibilities and, blinded by passion, is fooled by the *gracioso* Vigote—"Hazte Jael, que de noche / todos los gatos son pardos" (III, iv, pp. 298–99)—,[32] ["Disguise yourself as Jael, since at night / all cats are gray"]. The lust that both Sísara and Jabín feel for Jael, Heber Cineo's wife, their arrogance as well as the historic oppression of the Israelites by the Canaanites, send us to a time where injustice and disorder, as in colonial Peru, appear to be the dominant forces.

Such an age—the Canaanite for some spectators and the colonial for others—will cease to exist as portended by the signs that the European and Andean audience can recognize in the performance of the play. One could then argue that the ideological structure of *Amar* offers the world as it should be when it describes the end of tyranny, the rise of the underdogs on the social scale,[33] and the restoration of order as forecast by celestial signs. Just as the message learned from the Spanish play *Fuenteovejuna*—the right of the people to act against authority in the face of injustice—was well received by the public, the message of redemption given by *Amar* was equally gratifying to Indian and mestizo spectators. It could then be speculated that perhaps because of its mixed messages, *Amar* was consigned to oblivion and not performed outside the Dominican cloisters of San Antonio Abad. Viewed in this manner, the drama presents a curious paradox: in it the Baroque symbols are subverted by a Peruvian writer whose most cherished desire was to be accepted in European intellectual circles through the erudition that so clearly marked his writings.

The Female Protagonists

As has been pointed out, the dramatic nucleus of *Amar* revolves around two women: Jael, Heber Cineo's wife, loved by General Sísara and King Jabín; and Débora and her plans and prophecies. In fact, Jael pretends to accept Sísara's love in order to avenge the

Israelites; the plot thickens when Heber Cineo discovers that King Jabín has a portrait of his wife and thus senses that she has betrayed him. It is worth remembering now that Jael and Heber Cineo lived under the protection of the Canaanite king. Historically, the Book of Judges describes a period in which Israel lacked a common government, was attacked by other nations, and the various tribes fought among themselves (1220–1050 B.C.). The rulers were then called "judges" because they governed and judged as did Débora, the only woman that reached such a high rank; El Lunarejo deliberately selected this episode from the Book of Judges and placed Jael and Débora as the central figures of the drama. Did he do it because the situation in Israel was easily transferable to colonial Peru where Spanish laws brought chaos and the natural lords were supplanted by foreigners and Indians loyal to the Europeans?

The selection of two women as catalysts of the action[34] takes into account how the conduct of Jael and Débora could have been understood by the heterogeneous groups that conformed colonial society. It is well known that women warriors have a long and illustrious ancestry in Western and in Andean history where the deeds of *coyas*, or queens, and female leaders have been recorded. Let us remember, for example, the female rulers called *capullana* that in pre-Hispanic times ruled northern Peru; or Mama Huaco, the wife of the founder of the Inca empire, described as a strong and skillful warrior in one of the myths of origin of the Incas (Rostworoswki, 32–35, 131). Andean and European spectators could easily have identified with the admirable heroines selected by El Lunarejo.

In addition to underscoring the Baroque theme of the deceit of appearances and the deception of the senses, the actions of the female protagonists show how even the most vulnerable subjects are able to act and defeat powerful rulers. In the drama, Débora is vilified by Sísara on account of her gender; he says: "escuadras viles, / sujetas a bastones femeniles" ["vile squadrons, / under a woman's baton"] (I, i, p. 251). Nevertheless, Débora devises the plan that will destroy his army. Rejected by Barac who judges her to be a traitor, Jael offers hospitality to Sísara. Later she kills him by hammering a nail through his forehead while he is sleeping

(III, xvi, p. 319). At the end, she is honored for this deed that secured the triumph of the Israelites and her own vengeance. It is worth emphasizing that the variety of readings validated by the deeds of the female protagonists, are key elements in decentering the drama and giving it a fluidity that sharply contrasts with the rigidity of colonial society.

The fact that El Lunarejo selected Débora and Jael, the former as the moving force of the action and the latter as the agent for fulfilling the biblical prophecy, contradicts the traditional dynamic of the code of honor in which women were the victims. More importantly, the actions of the two female protagonists allow for a counter-cultural interpretation of the play in which the vanquished, using weapons and cunning, can defeat their oppressors. The humiliation of the latter is even greater when they are destroyed by those whom they disdained. It is worth underscoring that the conclusion of the drama safeguards the king because he was a friend of Heber Cineo, Jael's husband. Is this denouement a veiled criticism of the conduct of colonial authorities, particularly of Viceroy Francisco de Toledo who in 1572 ordered the beheading of Tupac Amaru, the last Inca king, in the main square of Cuzco?

Surely Native and European spectators could not but agree that the resolution proposed by *Amar* exemplifies the treatment owed to royalty even in times of armed conflict. At the same time, the cautious attitude of Jael, who pretends to live peacefully under the protection of her enemies while waiting for the proper moment to carry out her vengeance, shows a way of resistance very similar to the one proposed by Manco Inca when taking refuge in the stronghold of Vilcabamba (Titu Cusi Yupanqui, 26). In the *Relación* written by his son Titu Cusi, the Inca ruler advised his followers to tolerate the Spanish invaders while waiting for the opportune moment to defeat and expel them from Tahuantinsuyu.[35]

A review of the biography of Juan de Espinosa Medrano, showing his links to the Dominican and Jesuit orders, helps us to understand the author's interest in Native cultures and his wish to disseminate in Peru the best of Western thought in Spanish and Quechua. The fact that El Lunarejo, despite his talents, was at one time not properly recognized by the Church, and the constant envy of those who wanted to discredit him, contributed to developing in the author a consciousness of belonging to the periphery.

The exceptional erudition displayed in his works confirms the ambition of colonial writers to compare themselves with their Peninsular counterparts in order to show their equality and even their superiority. In the case of El Lunarejo, the process of appropriation of the imposed culture goes beyond this attitude. As Vargas Llosa has pointed out, "en vez de imitarla, pasa a crearla, aumentándola y renovándola" ["rather than imitating it [Western culture], he goes on to create it, expanding and renewing it"]. His daring position enhances the Baroque character of *Amar su propia muerte* expanding it with Andean elements. In this manner the drama opens a singular staging space from which it is possible to propose an antihegemonic interpretation of the play, thus revealing how Juan de Espinosa Medrano subverts the biblical narrative to question colonial order and affirm his own worth and that of his native land. Chapter 5 will take us back to the conquest of Peru in a drama in which Francisco del Castillo, informed by *Comentarios Reales* [*Royal Commentaries*] by the mestizo writer Garcilaso de la Vega, underscores the importance of Inca royalty in this event while diminishing the actions of Spanish soldiers. His play offers yet another interpretation of an event engraved in the collective consciousness of the Andean people.

5
Trespassing on Tradition: Francisco del Castillo's *La conquista del Perú*

INTRODUCTION

FRAY FRANCISCO DEL CASTILLO (1716–70), A POPULAR POET AND playwright of eighteenth-century Lima, was characterized by Ricardo Palma (1833–1919) as "Un loco más en el manicomio de las letras peruanas" ["Another maniac in the lunatic asylum of Peruvian literature]" (1957, 604). Several of Palma's articles established del Castillo's reputation as a shameless writer. The first one appeared in 1863 and collected amusing poems attributed to del Castillo, also known as the Ciego de la Merced [The Blind poet of the Mercedarian order],[1] and two other pieces turned up in the salacious collection *Tradiciones en salsa verde* [*Spicy Traditions*] not published until 1973.[2] They too refer to the licentious vein that, according to Palma, marked the poetry of Francisco del Castillo.

Palma's assertions have stimulated other critics to take an interest in this unique and multi-faceted writer of the colonial period. For example, the Peruvian historian Rubén Vargas Ugarte discovered and published in 1943 and 1948 several manuscripts by del Castillo.[3] The archival investigations of Guillermo Lohmann Villena, another historian, have provided accurate biographical information.[4] Recent research by literary critics has expanded our knowledge of the life and works of this prolific writer. Severo Aparicio discovered and published several poems by del Castillo, while Carlos Milla Batres devoted his doctoral dissertation to studying this author. Concepción Reverte Bernal analyzed the theater by the Ciego de la Merced in a book and several articles, and a critical edition of his plays. Based on this reevaluation of del Castillo's life and works, Daniel R. Reedy characterized his literary contribution as an important link in Peruvian satirical tradition, between the works of Juan del Valle Caviedes (c.1645-c.97) and Esteban de Terralla y Landa (?-1797?) (41–42).

The research on the life and works of Francisco del Castillo has confirmed his unusual talent as a poet and playwright. It has also revealed his attendance at weddings, bullfights, and parties, a world far removed from the cloisters of the Mercedarian order that he entered as a novice in 1733. At the same time, these studies have further confirmed del Castillo's connection to powerful figures of the viceregal court. Among them are: his literary patron, José Perfecto de Salas, a judge in Lima's Royal Tribunal; and Cristóbal Sánchez Calderón, Lima's inquisitor to whom he dedicated the religious play *Guerra es la vida del hombre* [*Man's Life is a Struggle*] (Reverte Bernal 1985a, 24). More recent studies have underscored other aspects of del Castillo's writing, specifically the religious character of some of his poetry and the wide spectrum of his theater. These analyses cast doubt on Palma's early assertions and call for a review of del Castillo's contribution to eighteenth-century Peruvian and Spanish American literature.

The Dramatic Production of Francisco del Castillo

Del Castillo's theater, made up of dramas, plays, interludes and one-act farces, occupies a unique position in colonial drama because of its volume and thematic diversity.[5] *Mitrídates, rey del Ponto* [*Mithridates, king of the Pontus*],[6] considered one of his major plays,[7] dramatizes the story of an obscure sovereign from Asia Minor subjugated by Rome. Four other major plays are: *El redentor no nacido, mártir, confesor y virgen: San Ramón* [*The Unborn Redeemer, Martyr, Confessor and Virgin: Saint Raymond*], and *Guerra es la vida del hombre* [*Man's Life is a Struggle*], both religious works; *Todo el ingenio lo allana* [*Wit Smooths Away Everything*], a comedy; and *La conquista del Perú* [*The Conquest of Peru*] (1748),[8] a historic play that, in my view, is the most interesting to modern readers on account of its theme and protagonists.

La conquista del Perú

This play and its *loa* or prologue were written at the request of the "gremio de los naturales" ["Indian guild"] of Lima to celebrate the coronation of Fernando VI in a celebration that took place in September of 1748, presided over by José Manso de Velasco, Count of Superunda and Viceroy of Peru (1745–61). An anonymous booklet, *El Día de Lima* [*Lima's Day*], published in 1748, described these festivities. They included artificial illumination and fireworks (216), the performance of *Ni amor se libra de amor* [*Not even Love Frees Itself from Love*] by the Spanish playwright Calderón de la Barca (224–25), and a "Fiesta de los naturales" ["Indian Festivity"] where Indians from Lima and surrounding areas paraded dressed as Inca nobles (237–68). While the booklet mentions that del Castillo wrote *La conquista del Perú* at the request of the Indian guild, it does not give details about its staging during the festivities.

Since in the last lines of his play del Castillo characterizes it as "famosa" ["famous"], it could be that either the play was performed or that, as was customary then, the author used the adjective to enhance its reputation. It must be noted that even though the final verse lines of the play mention a theater where "se ha visto / La conquista del Perú" ["has been seen / The conquest of Peru"], and that also the "senado" or public attending the performance (fol. 350r) approved of it with applause (Reverte Bernal 1985a, 180), there is no documentation corroborating its staging.

The main plot of *La conquista del Perú* fuses, as was frequent in Spanish Golden Age drama, three minor plots (Arrom 1967, 108–9). The first one is a love intrigue involving Inca princes and princesses: Titu Atauchi loves Mama Huaco, Mama Huaco loves Rumiñagüi, Rumiñagüi loves Huacolda, and Huacolda loves Culliscacha; the second subplot centers on the division of the Inca empire by Huayna Capac, the rivalry between Huascar and Atahualpa, Atahualpa's triumph and submission to the Spaniards; yet another intrigue revolves around the conquistadors, specifically Pedro de Candía and Francisco Pizarro who move from Panama to Isla del Gallo, and again to the mainland and the Inca cities of Tumbes, Cajamarca, and Cuzco. Following conventions of Golden Age drama, del Castillo concludes the play by joining the various secondary plots through the marriages of some of its characters. Approved by Francisco Pizarro, the conqueror of Peru, these unions appear to accept and celebrate the imposition of Spanish rule in the former Inca empire.

It should not surprise us that the author uses *Comentarios Reales* [*Royal Commentaries*] by Inca Garcilaso de la Vega as the principal historic source for this drama. This chronicle was published with a prologue by the Spanish historian Gabriel de Cárdenas (Andrés González de Barcia [1673–1743]) in a new edition in 1722 and 1723. It has been documented that this edition circulated widely in Peru.[9] In this regard, it is pertinent to remember a comment by the literary critic José Juan Arrom. He views *La conquista del Perú* as a reflection of the mentality shared by the author and its public, a frame of mind in the process of change due to the impact of the Enlightenment (1967, 109). The reading and discussion of *Comentarios Reales* [*Royal Commentaries*] by the criollo elite and the Inca nobility certainly acted as a catalyst for these changes. On the other hand, Reverte Bernal underscores the pro-Hispanic vision that leads del Castillo to alter history in three central episodes: the events at Cajamarca, the death of Huascar, and the swift submission of Atahualpa to the conquistadors (1985a, 182–81).

I would like to reassess the comments by these critics in order to present a different interpretation of *La conquista del Perú*. I propose that Francisco del Castillo, in his dramatization of the conquest, attempts to tarnish the brilliance of Spanish deeds in order to exalt Atahualpa, the Inca king garroted in Cajamarca, thus highlighting the contribution of the Incas in the creation of the new colonial order. Seen in this way, the play would also tenuously anticipate contradictions apparent in Andean criollo circles—love for the native land,[10] admiration for the glories of the Inca empire and their sovereigns,[11] desire to participate in the higher circles of colonial government, resentment of the privileges enjoyed by Spaniards,[12] rejection of the Indian masses. Thus, del Castillo's dramatic representation of the conquest of Peru would be in line with the irreverent attitude of his poetry which poked fun at colonial authorities and events.[13] At the same time, the author would follow colonial theatrical practices that included Native royalty as principal characters in order to present a different vision of events.[14] In this regard, it is important to underscore that during the eighteenth century the Incas and their descendants enjoyed great prestige as evidenced by several period engravings.[15] As Teresa Gisbert has aptly pointed out, the engravings had the following objective: to present a logical sequence of rulers from the Inca kings to the Spanish monarchs (1980, 129). Since these issues (criollo contradictions, an irreverent attitude, Native characters, the importance of Inca nobility at the time) are subtly intertwined in the drama, the spectators of *La conquista del Perú* could easily interpret its messages in a variety of ways. Let us now turn to some key events in the play in order to analyze how the author has highlighted them.

THE DEEDS OF A GREEK

It is well known that Pedro de Candía, a companion of Francisco Pizarro called "el griego" ["the Greek"] on account of his place of birth, was one of thirteen men that remained with the Spanish conquistador in Isla del Gallo, an island off the coast of Peru where he and his men nearly perished while waiting for reinforcements and supplies. According to Inca Garcilaso's *Comentarios Reales* [*Royal Commentaries*],[16] in an early exploration of the coast (1528), Candía dared to enter the port city of Tumbes. He was covered with a coat of mail, and carried a round shield in his left hand and a huge cross in his right hand. While in that city, the Natives brought a lion and a tiger to frighten him; however, the two animals were tamed by the sight of the cross and the natives welcomed Candía.[17] While in Tumbes, he noticed and reported the abundance of gold and silver in temple decorations, information used later to convince the Spanish sovereign to approve the conquest of Tahuantinsuyu. (See p. 103).

Del Castillo situates this episode at the center of the drama; he also underscores how the Indians believed that Candía was a god (fol. 329r). At the same time, he uses Candía and the Tumbes

Candía, the Greek artilleryman, in an imaginary conversation with Inca Huayna Capac (Guaman Poma [1615] 2:371). Courtesy of the editors.

episode to proclaim the rationality and worth of the Indians, meritorious of divine intervention: "también los indios hombres se llamaron, / redimidos también por [la Cruz de Cristo] fueron" ["also the Indians were called men / saved also by [the Cross of Christ]" (fol. 329v). In addition, the author proudly emphasizes that "la grandeza del Perú pregona / que del mundo es cabeza y es corona" ["the greatness of Peru proclaims / that of the world it is head and crown" (fol. 330r). This proud portrayal of his homeland by del Castillo is frequent in criollo writings depicting the grandeur of the Inca and Aztec empires, the beauty of American landscapes, the variety of the native flora and fauna, the splendors of colonial cities, and the wit of brainy criollos.[18]

Thus, Candía's episode fulfills several aims: 1) it stresses the rationality of Andeans; 2) it exalts the Inca past; and 3) assigns a key role to Candía, a Greek gunner, in the conquest of Tahuantinsuyu while displacing the Spaniards. It is worth remembering, however, that in Peru during the civil wars among the conquistadors (1541–54), Candía joined the rebels against the Crown and made several guns for them.[19] Indirectly, the drama raises an important question about the history of the colonial period: if the Spaniards entered Peru thanks to the deeds of a Greek artilleryman later turned rebel, who should be rewarded for the conquest of Tahuantinsuyu?

Predictions and Wonders

As in *Comentarios Reales* [*Royal Commentaries*] by Inca Garcilaso, the author includes in this drama the predictions of an ancient oracle forecasting the end of Inca rule with the arrival of strange beings on the coast of Peru (fols. 303v, 326r).[20] The drama also alludes to some of the wonders (the dead condor, earthquakes, comets, the three circles of the moon, sea swells) and predictions that in Huayna Capac's time augured a similar catastrophe. Key to the denouement of the drama are the allusions to Huayna Capac's last will and testament described in *Comentarios Reales* [*Royal Commentaries*]. There the Inca sovereign repeated the old omens and ordered his subjects to obey and serve the invaders because "en todo os harán ventaja; que su ley será mejor que la nuestra y sus armas poderosas e invencibles más que las vuestras" ["in everything they will be superior; their law will be better than ours and their weapons more powerful and invincible than ours"] (*Comentarios Reales* [*Royal Commentaries*] pt. 1, bk. 9, ch. 15, 250). Del Castillo sums up these ideas when he puts into poetry Garcilaso's version of Huayna Capac's last will and testament: (See pp. 106 and 107).

> Es, a saber, que a este Imperio
> vendrá una noble Nación,
> que os hará muchas ventajas
> en gobierno y en valor.
> A éstos os rendiréis luego
> sin mostrar alteración,
> siendo la obediencia ley
> a quien tendrá ley mejor.
> En mí el número se cumple
> de doce Reyes, que son
> los que están vaticinados
> por tanta declaración
> por los oráculos hecha,
> y así estad con prevención,
> no de armas, de rendimientos,
> que éste es decreto del Sol.
>
> (fol. 313v)

> [It is known that to this Empire
> will come a noble Nation,
> that will have great advantage
> over you in government and bravery.
> To this [nation] you will surrender
> without showing hesitation,
> as obedience is the first law
> for he who wishes to have a better law.
> In me the number has reached
> twelve kings, that are
> the ones prophesied
> by many statements
> made by the oracles
> and thus be on the alert
> not with weapons, but with devotion,
> for this the Sun has decreed.]

If one takes into account that the death of Huayna Capac and of his heir apparent, Ninan Cuyoche, was due to small-pox that

Inca Huayna Capac with the symbols of his authority (Guaman Poma [1615] 1:112). Courtesy of the editors.

The mummified body of Huayna Capac carried on a litter to Cuzco (Guaman Poma [1615] 2:379). Courtesy of the editors.

the Europeans brought to Mexico and from there traveled down the continent, the request for obedience to the invaders becomes ironic. The plea made by the Inca ruler becomes even more ironic as his own death and that of his heir apparent promoted the wars of "succession" between Huascar and Atahualpa, the weakening of Inca armies, the Spanish triumph in Cajamarca and later their entry in Cuzco, the capital of the Inca empire. Francisco del Castillo again chooses to follow *Comentarios Reales* [*Royal Commentaries*] to dramatize the conquest of Peru as a result of ancient predictions fully accepted by the Inca ruler in the firm belief that they will benefit his people. Following this argumentation, it is then possible to infer that the conquest of Tahuantinsuyu was due in part to the deeds of an untrustworthy Greek, but more directly to a divine design accepted and understood by the perceptive Huayna Capac. Thus the Spanish king owes the submission of the ancient empire to the Inca ruler and not to Pizarro and the conquistadors.[21] It is no wonder then that eighteenth-century engravings depicted a line of succession that went from the early Inca lords to the Spanish king, Fernando VI. The events staged in the drama would appear to conform to the line of succession depicted in the engravings. Both modes of representation bring to the fore yet another crucial question. Considering the contributions of Inca lords to the conquest of Peru, should they as well as those of European origin born in America, the criollos, have a right to participate in colonial government? One can be certain that this dangerous question, indirectly posed by the literature of the period, was frequently asked and affirmatively answered by Inca nobles and criollo intellectuals.

Atahualpa and his Dramatic Persona

In the play, another key character in the peaceful and reasoned surrender of Tahuantinsuyu is Atahualpa. In the presentation of this character it is important to note that when del Castillo dramatizes the narration of the division of the empire between Huascar and Atahualpa, the rivalries between the two, the treason of the latter, and the assassination of those belonging to noble Inca lineages from Cuzco (fols. 331–32), he again follows *Comentarios Reales* [*Royal Commentaries*]. However, in two dramatic moments—the Spanish arrival in Cajamarca and Atahualpa's quick surrender—the author draws away from that source in order to contrast Atahualpa's exemplary reasoning and qualities with the cruelty and marauding attributed to him.

Atahualpa's speech directed toward the conquistador Hernando de Soto helps us to understand del Castillo's depiction of the Inca sovereign. This speech reviews the ancient prophecies, particularly Huayna Capac's last will and testament, and comments on the failure of the "faraute" or interpreter to bridge the linguistic gap between Europeans and Andeans (fols. 343v–45r).[22] The speech makes evident that Atahualpa accepted the conquistadors; at the same time, it contrasts the cruelty of their actions with the peaceful welcome of the Inca lord:

> . . . , aunque llegasteis
> a nuestras tierras haciendo
> fatalidades y estragos,
> como lo lloran los nuestros,
> los toleramos pacientes,
> con realidad entendiendo
> que sois divinos y sois
> de nuestro dios mensajeros.
> . . . .
> se ha mandado por decreto
> que ninguno osado sea
> a violar vuestro respeto.
> Por tanto, podréis hacer
> lo que fuere gusto vuestro
> de nosotros, pues nosotros
> libre ofrenda nos hacemos;
> que harta gloria será nuestra
> morir a mano de aquéllos
> que, aunque inhumanos nos maten,
> por divinos los tenemos
> y veneramos, juzgando
> que son de Dios mensajeros.
> Que él sin duda os mandaría
> los estragos que habéis hecho,
> pues como sin culpa nuestra
> contra nosotros se hicieron,

infiero ser estas penas
por delitos contra el cielo.

(fols. 344r-v)

[. . . , even though you arrived
in our lands
killing and destroying,
and our people cried over this,
we patiently tolerated you
in reality understanding
that you are divine beings and are
messengers of our god.
. . . .
It has thus been decreed
that no one may dare
to disrespect you.
Thus, you can do
whatever pleases you
with us, because we
offer ourselves freely;
it will be to our glory
to die at the hands of those
who, even if they inhumanely kill us,
but we view and revere them
as divine, judging
that they are God's messengers.
For he without a doubt ordered
the havoc that you have done,
because as we were innocent
and against us it was committed,
I assume these punishments
to be for crimes against heaven.]

As has been pointed out previously, the words of Atahualpa confirm the voluntary submission of the Andeans and focus on the divine character of the Europeans. More importantly, the speech underscores Atahualpa's magnanimity when peacefully welcoming the conquistadors; it also exonerates the Spaniards by attributing their cruel actions to divine punishment deserved by the Inca and his people for previously committed "crimes against heaven." Del Castillo takes advantage of this exchange between Atahualpa and de Soto to contrast the misdeeds of the invaders with the peaceful reception given them by Atahualpa and the Andeans.[23]

Two other parts of this speech are fundamental to our interpretation of *La conquista del Perú* [*The Conquest of Peru*]. On the one hand, an Inca sovereign, Atahualpa, occupies a central space in the drama as he welcomes the invaders. This emphasizes once more Atahualpa's key role in the incorporation of the Inca empire to Spanish dominion and also diminishes the heroic deeds of the Spanish conquistadors. In addition, the speech criticizes the cruelty of the Spaniards. Perhaps this characterization of the excessive actions of the invaders placed in a central scene of the drama, forecasts the subtle change of mentality noticed by Arrom in the literature of eighteenth-century Spanish America. An aside by the *gracioso* [*comic character*] Llupanguillo would tend to confirm it. His speech points to the economic gains of the conquest for the Europeans mockingly characterized as "espantajos" [scarecrows]:

> ¡Oiga!, ¿fruta les traen ahora
> a estos espantajos nuevos [los invasores]?;
> ¡linda cosecha tendrán
> con los frutos del Imperio!
>
> (fol. 342v)

> [Listen!, you now bring fruit
> to these new scarecrows [the invaders]?;
> they will have a bountiful crop
> with the fruits of the Empire!]

Such comments at best are conflicting if one takes into account that in *La conquista del Perú* [*The Conquest of Peru*], "el gremio de los naturales" ["the Indian guild"] of Lima expresses its "cordial, reverente obsequio" ["cordial, reverent gift"] (fol. 300r) to the Catholic King Fernando VI whose coronation in 1748 will assure the continuity of the Spanish monarchy and its rule over the Indies.

If to this we add that in the *loa* or prologue to the play a dialogue between Nación Peruana [Peruvian Nation] and Europa [Europe], two allegorical characters, as well as references to the links between Inca and Spanish nobility through the marriage of Martín García de Loyola and Beatriz Clara Coya in Cuzco (see chapter 1), help to reaffirm the equality of Europe and Peru,[24] it would be plausible to assert that *La conquista del Perú* [*The Conquest of Peru*] foreshadows the contradictory views of the criollo elite. This privileged group admired ancient Amerindian civilizations and rejected common Indians and other *castas*.[25]

Atahualpa's Capture

A central act in the conquest of Peru as portrayed in history and in the play is the encounter of Europeans and Andeans in Cajamarca and the subsequent capture of Atahualpa. It is well known that in this key encounter, thousands of Andeans were killed while the invaders suffered no losses (Lockhart 1986, 1:23–24). The author offers an exceptional version of this event in which the submission of the Andeans is achieved through the intervention of the Inca. In fact, while Atahualpa questions the effectiveness of the interpreter, an altercation among Spaniards and Indians interrupts the action. Inca Atahualpa stands up and says:

> A los españoles nadie
> les toque ni aun el vestido,
> aunque me prendan y maten;
> miren que es precepto mío.

(fol. 348v)

> [Let no one touch
> even the clothing of the Spaniards,
> even if I am captured and killed;
> this is my command.]

And accepting the ancient predictions, he concludes:

> Ya esto no tiene remedio,
> ya el fin del Imperio mío
> ha llegado, de mi padre
> cumplióse ya el vaticinio;
> mas, pues tienen ley mejor
> estos hombres que han venido,

por ganar mejor imperio
abrasarla determino.

(fol. 348v)

[Nothing can be done,
the end of my empire
has come, my father's
prediction has been realized
however, they have a better law,
those men that have arrived,
to gain a worthier empire
I am determined to embrace it.]

Following this speech, the Inca king rejects his ancient beliefs, is baptized, and requests to be absolved from his responsibility in Huascar's death (fol. 349r). In this key scene, the conqueror Pizarro and the priest Valverde appear as secondary characters while Atahualpa plays a principal role. In addition, from the point of view of the dominant culture, the Inca king is vindicated when his previous "tiranías" ["tyrannies"] are forgiven by his acceptance of Christianity and Spanish rule. It is my contention that the author uses this scene to cast a shadow on European heroic deeds in order to underscore that the Crown owes two Incas—Huayna Capac and Atahualpa—the conquest of Tahuantinsuyu.[26] Is it that del Castillo is insinuating that this debt should be paid and thus the Inca elite should have a right to govern, or perhaps even claim, the territory given to Spain by their ancestors?

A Happy Ending?

It was pointed out at the outset that *La conquista del Perú* [*The Conquest of Peru*] closes with the standard marriages that in Golden Age theater signaled the return to the prevalent social order. In this case Mama Huaco and Titu, characters in one of the subplots, are married; Huacolda, another character of the secondary plot, remains alone when she demands that Rumiñagüi, her partner, convert to Christianity. To this he answers: "Eso después lo veremos, / que tengo que hacer en Quito" ["We will see about that later, / I have things to attend to in Quito"] (fol. 350r). It is significant that the author brings to the fore this historic character. The record shows that Rumiñagüi or Rumiñahui allied himself with Atahualpa in the struggle for the Inca throne. After the Inca was captured in Cajamarca on 16 November 1532, Rumiñagüi took refuge in Quito where it is believed that he ordered the killing of Yllescas, another brother of Atahualpa and also a contender for the throne of the Inca empire. Rumiñagüi later fought against the invaders and their allies, the Cañari Indians, commanded by Sebastián de Benalcázar (?-1551); later he was apprehended, and burned alive by order of Benalcázar. Inca Garcilaso confirms Rumiñagüi's retreat to Quito and his obstinate resistance to Spanish rule (*Comentarios Reales* [*Royal Commentaries*] pt. 2, bk. 1, ch. 28). The Andean chronicler Guaman Poma de Ayala describes him as a daring warrior and also as a traitor and murderer because he killed Inca Yllescas in Quito (1:143).[27]

In our interpretation of this drama, Rumiñagüi's retreat and his refusal to accept Christianity offer the drama an open ending where waiting for the right moment to act could be viewed as an alternative way to resist and survive colonial rule. Rumiñagüi's cautious comment, "Eso después lo veremos" ["We will see about that later"] (fol. 350r) invites a judgment of the invaders. It is not accidental then that in the drama, a rebel—Rumiñagüi—refuses to accept the imposition of Spanish rule in the Andes symbolized by his marriage to Huacolda.[28] As they are dramatized in the play, these attitudes and deeds could be interpreted as worthy of emulation by the spectators. However, the missing historic information about the fate of the rebel Rumiñagüi, conveys the high price he paid for his actions as well as the swift and cruel manner in which Spanish justice was dispensed—Rumiñagüi was killed for his rebellion against the Crown. (See p. 115).

With subtle irreverence Francisco del Castillo constructs in his drama a peculiar image of the conquest of Peru. Almost imperceptibly, it incorporates rebellion as a fact of the past and perhaps a possibility for the future. It also insinuates that the heroic deeds of conquistadors were fabrications, and their cruelties unnecessary as the Inca empire was freely given to them by the will and testament of Huayna Capac and the actions of Atahualpa. By depicting the Incas in this manner, the author brings to the center

The rebel leader Rumiñagüi (Guaman Poma [1615] 1:165). Courtesy of the editors.

of the stage and of history a civilization respected and admired by many members of the criollo elite. In so doing, del Castillo subtly brings out issues related to the role and rights of Inca and criollo elites. All of this incorporated in a drama written to honor Fernando VI at the request of an Indian guild from Lima, reveals the many complexities hidden behind the facade of viceregal dramatic works. During the eighteenth century, writers, either willingly or inadvertently trespassed on tradition as they wrote between two critical moments: the lengthy colonial rule and the rupture that the Enlightenment philosophy would bring about.

Conclusion

LITERARY CRITICS HAVE LONG EXAMINED THE PRINCIPAL ROLE played by drama in the evangelization of the native population and in providing a means of cross-cultural communication. However, the unique messages sent by these plays to heterogeneous viewers have not been as well researched. In the preceding pages, I have argued that drama creates an arena where foreign and native cultures clash and converge. The stage evolves as a singular "library" on which visual and linguistic signs representing different world views release messages. These messages have different meanings for the criollo elite, the indigenous population and the growing number of *castas*.

The dramatic works that have been analyzed offer a representative corpus allowing us to explore these dissimilar messages. *Tragedia del fin de Atahualpa* shows the lasting impact of the conquest on the collective memory of the Andean people. The various dramatic versions of this event as well as its contemporary staging in religious and patriotic celebrations, take us back to the rupture first brought about by the imprisonment of Atahualpa and, then, by the beheading of Tupac Amaru I. In the version of the play that was examined, the concept of poetic justice, characteristic of Spanish Golden Age drama, permeates the tragedy in its attempt to close the historic and cultural gap. In this way, by linking Spanish dramatic style and native history, the playwright produces a work of a heterogeneous nature. It projects the clash of cultures and the possibility of accommodating their different universes—the American in its Andean modality and the European in its Peninsular expression.

It has been widely accepted that as of the last decades of the seventeenth century to the late eighteenth century many plays were written in Quechua, and *Usca Paucar* is one of these works.

Through the use of the popular European theme of selling one's soul to the devil, its Indian protagonist brings out the predicament of the indigenous subjects of the Spanish empire. In creating this peculiar juncture, the writer of the Quechua play gives new meaning to an old motif. *Amar su propia muerte* by Juan de Espinosa Medrano, behind its traditional facade of using a biblical episode, also points, albeit indirectly, to colonial reality. In this work the protagonist Jael is a woman whose actions manifest the possibility of rebellion against injustice even by the helpless. Characterized by Baroque symbols and metaphors whose connections to Andean reality appear remote, the hidden message of this drama slowly reveals itself. In both *Usca Paucar* and *Amar su propia muerte* traditional themes acquire irreverent meanings by reworking religious and Baroque symbols and referring the viewers to a concrete colonial reality.

The use of Andean history as a constant in theater is illustrated by *La conquista del Perú* [*The Conquest of Peru*], an eighteenth-century play by Francisco del Castillo. This drama, confirming the impact of *Comentarios Reales* [*Royal Commentaries*] by Inca Garcilaso de la Vega on the viceroyalty of Peru, shows how the criollo elite manipulated Inca history to discreetly question Spanish supremacy in Peru and insert themselves in real and virtual historical events.

The analysis of these dramas emphasizes the significance and richness of theater in the Andean world. By decoding the hidden messages of these plays and ascertaining their impact and by understanding why the dramas privilege Andean history while reshaping Peninsular dramatic praxis, students of Spanish America's colonial period will find many fresh insights into a complex literary legacy and cultural reality.

Notes

Chapter 1. Movable Meanings: Evangelization, Literacy, and Missionary Theater

1. See Lienhard 29–53, 99–123.
2. Gaspar Antonio Chi, a Mayan nobleman educated by the missionaries, assisted Landa in learning the language and culture of the region. About Chi, see Karttunen (84–114).
3. In this regard see Lockhart (1992, 405–7).
4. Among the teachers of this singular institution is Bernardino de Sahagún (1529–90). With the help of bilingual and trilingual native informants, Sahagún began to study the Nahuatl language and to collect information about the philosophy, religion, science, and literature of the Nahua people. Of all the manuscripts that Sahagún and his assistants so carefully gathered, only *Psalmodia christiana y sermonario de los sanctos del año en lengua mexicana* (1583), a book of religious instruction, appeared during his lifetime. Sahagún's encyclopedic *Historia general de las cosas de Nueva España* [*General History of the Things from New Spain*] was not published until the nineteenth century.
5. For a review of these books see Resines Llorente.
6. John B. Glass has reviewed the Testerian manuscripts.
7. For an overview of missionary theater in Mexico see Arróniz.
8. Translations into English of this and other quoted material are mine.

Chapter 2. Historical and Cultural Contentions in *Tragedia del fin de Atahualpa*

1. For example, the dances of the Inca king and the Spanish captain performed in different towns of central Peru also recreate and reinterpret the events of Cajamarca (see Burga).
2. Another well known version is a Quechua-Spanish drama presented in the city of Oruro (Bolivia) and published by C. H. Balmori in 1955; in 1943 Teodoro Meneses discovered and translated another drama of this cycle which he later published (see Meneses 1987).
3. The quotes are from Lara's bilingual edition. There is a revised version of this translation into Spanish (see Meneses 1983).
4. In this regard, it is worth observing that the drama of the confrontation of Andeans and Europeans, symbolized by the imprisonment and death of Atahualpa, has not gone unnoticed by other writers. For example, the British playwright Peter Shaffer based his *The Royal Hunt of the Sun* on these historical events. This British play enhances Atahualpa's personality and god-like qualities

in such a way that it also conveys the message of hope and salvation so evident in Andean dramas of the so-called Atahualpa cycle.

5. Alberto Flores Galindo and Manuel Burga have recognized the importance of this theme and have studied it from historic and anthropological perspectives.

6. Another important leader of this rebellion was Julián Apasa Tupac Catari (c. 1750–81). This Indian leader, from what is now Bolivia, organized the army that on two occasions laid siege to La Paz. Tupac Catari declared himself viceroy of Tupac Amaru II and did not accept the royal pardon. He was later imprisoned and executed.

7. Surely the admiration and respect that the Andeans felt for the last Inca made this and other leaders claim to be descendants of Atahualpa. About this, see Arzáns de Orsúa (1:99).

8. At the beginning of the revolt, an English squadron commanded by Admiral George Anson (1697–1762) was sighted off the coast of Peru. However, this squadron was sent to attack Pacific ports because England had declared war on Spain in 1739 (Tauro 1:139–40).

9. Durand explains that Tupac Amaru II was a devoted reader of the *Comentarios Reales* [*Royal Commentaries*]. For this literary critic, the Andean leader found in this book "la biblia secreta" ["the secret Bible"] of the 1780 revolution (208). José Antonio del Busto has proposed that Tupac Amaru read the *Comentarios Reales* [*Royal Commentaries*] while a student at the Colegio de San Francisco de Borja in Cuzco, a school created in the seventeenth century to educate the sons of Inca nobility and of important "caciques" (45–46). In fact, probably due to their Jesuit training, the "caciques" were able to read the work of their compatriot and to understand the parts in Latin of the suggestive "Prólogo" by González de Barcia to the eighteenth-century edition (Rowe 1954, 26). Regarding the diffusion of the *Comentarios Reales* in Peru, see Guibovich 1992.

10. It is known that Tupac Amaru II saw a performance of the drama *Ollantay* before his rebellion. In addition, in the nineteenth-century copies of earlier dramas written in Quechua still circulated—*Huascar Inca, Titu Cusi Yupanqui*. Today only the titles remain (Rowe 1954, 31).

11. I had the opportunity of consulting a copy of the eighteenth-century edition of the *Comentarios Reales* [*Royal Commentaries*] in The John Carter Brown Library.

12. According to González de Barcia, these priests brought a "Book of the *Gospels*" illustrated with the "Casos" of the Articles of Faith.

13. In a note to their critical edition of *Primer nueva corónica* [*First New Chronicle*], Murra and Adorno interpret this mixture of famous figures as an allegory of the discovery of America (2:375).

14. González de Barcia presented the prophecy in a translation from Latin done by Theodor de Bry (Rowe 1954, 26).

15. Raleigh indicates: "And I further remember, that Berreo [Antonio de Berrio, governor of Trinidad] confessed to me and others, . . . that there was found among prophecies in Peru (at such time as the empire was reduced to the Spanish obedience) in their chiefest temples, amongst diverse others which foreshewed the loss of the said empire, that from Inglatierra those Ingas should be again in time to come restored, and delivered from the servitude of the said [Spanish] conquerors" (467). Did Berrio tell the English sailor this prophecy, or did Raleigh invent it in order to convince the Queen of England to finance first the conquest of Guyana, and later that of Peru? (Rowe 1954, 26–27). In this

regard, it is worth remembering that in the same book Raleigh had explained that Guyana and its territories were so rich and advanced because its emperor was a descendant of the Incas. Thus Guyana was ruled by the same laws and practiced the same religion as Tahuantinsuyu: "one of the younger sons of Guaynacapa fled out of Peru, and took with him many thousands of those soldiers of the empire called Oreiones, and with those, and many others which followed him, he vanquished all that tract and valley of America which is situate[d] between the great rivers of Amazonez and Baraquan, otherwise called Oroonoko and Maranion" (397–98).

16. According to legend, Tupac Amaru's head was displayed publicly and it grew more beautiful with time. Burga asks if, in fact, the myth of Inkarrí begins with this legend (118–20). It is known that the king's head quickly began to be worshipped by the Indians. That is why Viceroy Toledo ordered that it be buried with the body the day after Tupac Amaru was beheaded (Zimmerman 1968, 114).

17. The painting is housed in the Museo Inca (formerly the Museo Arqueológico), Cuzco, Peru.

18. López Baralt has done a comprehensive study of the meaning of the black rainbow with reference to the elegy "Al todopoderoso Inca Atahualpa" ["To the Mighty Inca Atahualpa"] (1987, 37–84).

19. In the sixteenth and seventeenth centuries there were other movements of salvation and liberation such as the *muru onqoy* [sickness of the spots] of 1590, so named because it coincided with a plague, and two others in Arequipa (1660) and Vilcas (1656) related to earthquakes and volcanic eruptions (López Baralt 1987, 18; Espinoza Soriano, 143–52).

20. The first dealt with the origin of the Incas and the deeds of Manco Capac; the second with Huayna Capac's victory; the third depicted Huascar's coronation and the struggle between the two brothers; the fourth play was about the arrival of the Spaniards and the death of Atahualpa (Arzáns de Orsúa, 1:98).

21. A northern territory part of today's Ecuador, pacifically incorporated into the Inca empire by Tupac Inca Yupanqui. Inca lore represents the Cañari people as untrustworthy outsiders. Historically the Cañaris joined the Spaniards and together they fought the Incas and their descendants; as a result, they were rewarded with certain privileges in colonial Peru.

22. After his defeat (1537), Manco Inca abandoned Cuzco and took refuge with his followers in the mountains of Vilcabamba.

23. We know that historically this meeting was impossible since Pizarro's comrade-in-arms did not arrive in Cajamarca until 12 April 1533.

24. See, for example, the one edited and translated by Balmori.

25. About poetic justice, see Parker.

26. In a letter to Pizarro, the king of Spain, Charles V, expresses his disapproval of the conquistador's sentencing of Atahualpa because it was illegal according to the laws governing a royal institution (Rostworowski, 177).

27. In this regard it is worth noting that Pedro Pizarro (1515–87), in his *Relación del descubrimiento y conquista de los reinos del Perú* (1571), explains that the Inca "había hecho entender a sus hermanos y mujeres que si no le quemaban volvería a este mundo . . ." ["had made his brothers and wives understand that if he was not burned, he would return to this world"]. This is why, according to Pizarro, the king was first executed and then burned. The Spanish conquerors publicized and manipulated this last fact in order to dispel any popular hopes

for the return of the Inca (see Balmori, 46; Burga, 79). Atahualpa's body, after its burial in a church, disappeared and has never been found (Rostworowski, 176).

28. During the international congress "Los mundos del Inca Garcilaso" (Madrid, 2–6 April 1990), María Rostworowski confirmed how zealously the Andeans guarded the *mallqui* from the searches sponsored by the priests. In addition to the preservation of the body, other important burial rites among the Incas were songs and dances retelling the deeds of the deceased and expressing the hope for their return (Burga, 77–78).

29. Regarding the presence of the past in the Andes and its permanence and vitality in contemporary artistic and literary manifestations, see Castro-Klarén 1990.

30. These interpretations have been disputed by contemporary historians (see Levillier, and Zimmerman 1968). Viceroy Toledo arrived in Spain on 15 September 1581 after having ruled Peru for more than thirteen years. He died on 21 April 1582 in the village of Escalona. Even though it is impossible to know details of the conversation between the king and his viceroy, it is known that judgment on the financial aspects of Toledo's tenure in Peru was so complicated that the Royal Council of the Indies and other officials of the Crown in Spain and abroad studied them for sixteen years, thus delaying the rewards and privileges requested by his descendants (Zimmerman 1968, 273–75).

CHAPTER 3. THE INTERFACE OF RELIGIOUS AND SCENIC ARTS IN THE QUECHUA PLAY *USCA PAUCAR*

1. Information on an earlier translation of the *Faust-Buch* now lost, has made it possible to speculate on another date of composition, 1588–89, for this work by Marlowe. See the textual introduction by Bowers (123–324), in his edition of *Doctor Faustus*.

2. It has been attributed to the Cuzcan priest Juan de Espinosa Medrano (1629?-88). About this writer see chapter 4.

3. Meneses gives dates of composition and authorship of both works in his *Teatro quechua colonial. Antología* (165–76; 375–84). Vasco de Contreras occupied important ecclesiastical posts, served as rector of the University of San Marcos (1653–54), and later Bishop of Popayán (1658–65). He died on his way to Ayacucho, the seat of his new bishopric.

4. During the 27th International Congress of Americanists held in Lima in 1939, Valcárcel made known another codex of *Usca Paucar*, more complete than the one disseminated by Middendorf (Meneses 1983, 169).

5. All quotes are from this edition; the corresponding act, scene and page are indicated in parentheses.

6. This codex survived the fire of 1943 in the Biblioteca Nacional. Its 1,760 verses, divided into three acts, are copied double-spaced on thirty-two pages of cardboard bound in the tome *Literatura incásica* (pp. 139–70), by Justo Apu Sahuaraura. The copy bears the date of 4 September 1838 and is signed by Sahuaraura Inca (Meneses 1983, 170). It also includes *Ollantay*, another famous Quechua play. Thanks to Ella Dunbar Temple's research, we know that Justo Apu Sahuaraura Ramos Tito Atauchi (c. 1775-c.1853) was a descendant of Inca nobility who became a priest, joined the cause of independence starting with the rebellion led in 1814 by Mateo Pumacahua, and later followed the army commanded by Sucre in the battle of Ayacucho in 1824. It seems that he also

wrote and compiled a series of historic documents that were later catalogued under the title of *Literatura incásica*, where he included *Usca Paucar*. He is the author of *Recuerdos de la monarquía peruana, o Bosquejo de la historia de los incas* [*Memoirs of the Peruvian Monarchy, or Outline of the History of the Incas*], a work that was printed in Paris in 1850, and which contains sixteen portraits from the imperial dynasty.

7. The Jesuits (1568) stand out for their evangelization among the indigenous elite.

8. About these performances during Inca times, see the works of Bolivian linguist and literary critic, Jesús Lara.

9. His *Grammática o Arte de la lengua general de los Indios del Reyno del Perú* [*Grammar of the General Language of the Indians from the Kingdom of Peru*] and *Lexicón o Vocabulario de la lengua general del Perú* [*Vocabulary of the General Language of Peru*] were published in 1560 in Valladolid.

10. The best known and most complete of these early dictionaries is the *Vocabulario de la lengua general de todo el Perú, llamada lengua quichu o del Inca* [*Vocabulary of the General Language in the Whole of Peru, Known as Quichua or Language of the Inca*] (1608), by Diego González de Holguín (1552–1618).

11. See the text of the *Sínodo quitense. Constituciones para curas de indios* (1570), which López Baralt discusses. In this text priests were instructed to explain to their indigenous parishioners that the images are of writing (López Baralt 1988, 173). Regarding Andean religious views see MacCormack; about indigenous perceptions of Christianity and the actions of the missionaries see Mills.

12. Probably oil paintings on small panels brought in the baggage of members of religious orders (Tord 1989, 168).

13. Diego Quispe Tito (1611–81) and Basilio Santa Cruz Pumacallao (?-?) were two outstanding Indian artists during this period. In 1688, the rivalries that separated Spanish and criollo painters from Indians and mestizo painters gave rise to a distinct pictorial style—that of the famous Cuzco school (Gisbert 1986a, 26–27).

14. It was edited and published by Fray Arturo Alvarez under the title *Un viaje fascinante por la América Hispana del siglo XVI* (Madrid, 1969) (Mesa and Gisbert 1977, 46).

15. See Teresa Gisbert's edition of this devotional book.

16. This process has been studied in colonial painting by Teresa Gisbert (1980, 17–22). A similar syncretism occurred in Cuba with the Virgen de la Caridad del Cobre (see Arrom 1971, 184–214).

17. Also in 1605 Pope Paul V grants, over a period of fifteen years, 150 indulgences to those who listened to the *Salve* and litanies while kneeling in the churches of Peru (Vargas Ugarte 1947, 55–56).

18. Among the devotional works, the *Symbolo Cathólico Indiano*, by Luis Gerónimo de Oré (1554–1630), a Franciscan native of Guamanga [today Ayacucho], contains canticles written in Quechua and Aymara and annotated in Latin. In these the central character is sometimes the Virgin Mary. It is important to recall that, as already noted, the models for the characters in later religious Quechua theater probably originated in sacred verse (Beyersdorff 1988, 18). As for the shrines, the one in Pomata, under the care of the Dominicans, was dedicated to the Virgin of the Rosary, whose attributes were considered the same as those of the Virgin of Pomata by the middle of the seventeenth century (Gisbert 1980, 83). Since this order was in charge of the sodalities of Indians and Blacks devoted

to the Rosary, the Virgin of Pomata was frequently regarded as the protectoress of both groups.

19. Among them Santa María de la Peña de Francia or Nuestra Señora de la Peña de Francia.

20. The relationship between Our Lady of the Rock of France and that of the Virgin of Copacabana, colonial painting and the illustrations of *Primer nueva corónica* [*First New Chronicle*] has been studied by Mercedes López Baralt (1988, 271–90).

21. The description is given in Spanish in Middendorf's edition as well as in Sahuaraura's manuscript.

22. For the "souls" or aides of the Devil, the beads of the rosary are sharp thorns (II, xii, p. 145).

23. Michael, Gabriel and Raphael are from the Bible; Uriel, Jehudiel, Barachiel and Seathiel, or Seactiel, are barely mentioned in the apocryphal books.

24. Pope Clement X (1670–76) officialized this devotion to the Guardian Angel.

25. An apocryphal book of Enoch records the names and functions of the angels, for example, "Bardiel, angel-prince of hail" (Gisbert 1980, 86). See also Herzberg.

26. Regarding its origin and novelty, see Herzberg.

27. "Pin Dios Jhina; nojamanta" ["Who is like God"] (I, ii, p. 49), or "Who like God," that comes from the Hebrew word for Michael.

28. In these shields the litanies of Mary were inscribed (Gisbert 1986b, 61).

29. For a more detailed study of the theme, see Gutiérrez.

Chapter 4. Expanding Baroque Boundaries in *Amar su propia muerte* by Juan de Espinosa Medrano

1. Meneses published the Spanish version of this play using a codex that the historian Luis E. Valcárcel made known in 1939 (1983, 91–163). Luis Jaime Cisneros pointed out the problems presented by the lack of original manuscripts of Espinosa Medrano's plays (1995, 1677–78).

2. In the Andean region the name of Pedro de Peralta Barnuevo Rocha y Benavides (Lima, 1663–1743) comes to mind.

3. During the eighteenth century, Diego de Esquivel y Navia and Ignacio de Castro had referred to Espinosa Medrano's Indian heritage (see Cisneros and Guibovich 1988; González Boixo 1997).

4. The complete Spanish title is: *Discurso sobre si en un concurso de opositores a beneficio curado debe ser preferido* caeteris paribus *el beneficiado al que no lo es en la promoción de dicho beneficio* [*Discourse on the topic of who should be rewarded with the position in a competition for ecclesiastical office, the person that placed his name in the competition or a person nominated for the position by others*].

5. Some of these comments were later omitted from the second edition (Lima, 1694) of this work.

6. I thank Elias Rivers and Georgina Sabat de Rivers for providing bibliographical information about this article and later sending a complete copy.

7. Quotations from the *Apologético* are from the edition prepared by José Carlos González Boixo (1997); it follows the first edition of the work printed in Lima by Quevedo y Zárate in 1662. Quotations from *La lógica* correspond to the Biblioteca Ayacucho edition prepared by Augusto Tamayo Vargas.

8. In the anonymous Prologue to *La novena maravilla* [*The Ninth Marvel*], a collection of his sermons, the author, probably Antonio Cortéz de la Cruz, a former disciple of El Lunarejo, comments: "Pero quien dixera, que vn hombre tan eminente, vn tan grande Theologo, como aquel huviesse quienes lo quisiessen apocar despues de su muerte, de tal manera, que se dexaron dezir: Que no era tanto que supo, y que aun en la Theologia fue ignorante, . . . Si bien no fuera hombre grande, a no tener emulos que acometiesen deslustrarle, ó embidiosos, o incredulos de su fama" ["But who would say that there were those that wanted to diminish such an eminent man and great theologian after his death. They even dare to say: He did not know that much, and that even of Theology he was ignorant. . . . If he were not such a great man, there would not be those that wish to blemish his reputation, or envious persons, or those that did not believe that he [Espinosa Medrano] was so famous"] (6v).

9. González Echevarría views him as the "baroque gentleman" characterized earlier by the Cuban writer José Lezama Lima (*Celestina's Brood*, 150).

10. A decree issued by Viceroy Francisco de Toledo on 7 July 1579, authorized the creation of a Chair in Quechua at the University of San Marcos. Studies of viceregal libraries during the colonial period confirm the many interests of Peruvian intellectuals. See, for example, the inventory of Bishop Hernando Arias de Ugarte (Hampe Martínez, 336–61), and of a private library in seventeenth-century Cuzco (Cisneros and Guibovich 1982, 141–71).

11. Luis Jaime Cisneros has explained the characteristics of sermons collected in *La novena maravilla* [*The Ninth Marvel*], emphasizing that they were intended for a highly educated group of listeners (1984, 4). On the other hand, it has been pointed out that, since the general public did not understand the religious message when clothed in such verbal complexities, they received the message through emotion and not reason (Rodríguez Garrido, 18).

12. During the early years of the colonial period mestizos were easily admitted to the religious orders. In 1578, however, a Royal Decree forbade their admittance to these orders (Tibesar, 33). After an appeal by mestizo priests, the decree was revoked in 1588. Even though the Crown did not view with favor the ordination of mestizos, many opted for an ecclesiastical career as it was one of the few paths to economic and social advancement.

13. The descendants of the Incas were loyal to the Jesuits before they established the schools for caciques. There is evidence that in Cuzco, in May of 1610, before the town council and other authorities, the Indian nobility declared as their patron saint the recently beatified Saint Ignatius of Loyola, the founder of the Order (Esquivel y Navia, 2:11).

14. For a review of the curriculum and daily activities in San Francisco de Borja during the middle of the eighteenth century, see del Busto 43–45.

15. The Jesuits also founded San Ignacio de Loyola (1622), the first university in Cuzco.

16. In 1692 this school became a university.

17. His links to the Dominican order have been studied (see Cisneros 1989, 248).

18. About the "Jesuit empire" and their missions in Mojos, Chiquitos and Paraguay, see Mörner.

19. The Jesuits organized their students patterned on the Roman army. They were divided into groups of ten under the direction of a "decurion" who assisted the teacher. Each group prepared dramatic representations with a small number of characters (Vargas Ugarte 1974, xxx–iv).

20. For example, it is known that in the festivities organized in Lima (1596) to welcome Viceroy Luis de Velasco, the Jesuits sponsored the performance of *Historia alegórica del Anticristo y el Juicio Final* [*Allegorical Story of the AntiChrist and the Final Judgment*]; in order to enhance the final scene of the Resurrection, they unearthed mummies from Indian sacred places close to Lima and placed them on the stage (Arrom 1967, 32).

21. About Jesuit drama also see Arrom (1967, 32–35).

22. In Cuzco, construction for its first theater began in 1622. According to Esquivel y Navia, construction lasted more than ninety years; however, it was mainly used for "otros juegos" ["other entertainments"] (Esquivel y Navia, 2:46).

23. All quotes from this play are from the Biblioteca Ayacucho edition.

24. The final verses of the play clarify that Espinosa Medrano "la sacó a luz" ["brought it to light"] when he was a student in the Dominican seminary of San Antonio Abad (III, xvi, p. 322).

25. The historian Rubén Vargas Ugarte published it under the pseudonym Juan del Rimac in *Revista de la Universidad Católica del Perú* (1932–34); several years later (1943) the piece was reprinted in a collection of Peruvian colonial theater also edited by this historian.

26. For more details about the concept of hybridism and its importance in colonial literatures, see Bhabha.

27. Josefina Ludmer has called these strategies "tretas del débil" ["tricks of the weak"] (53). My thanks to Alberto Sandoval for referring me to this article.

28. The most common was the division in four parts or quarters.

29. Billie Jean Isbell has studied this distribution of space and shown that it is prevalent today.

30. The appearance of the comet is followed by an owl, a bird generally identified with night and death in the Western tradition inherited from Egypt (Cirlot, 247). In the Andean world the "graznido" of this bird forecasts death (Rowe 1963, 304). Guaman Poma draws owls of two sizes among the animals that can cause misfortunes (1:283).

31. The *acco chinchay* alludes to comets flying; the *tapiya ccuyllur* or *tapiyacuyllur* can be translated as the "threatening comet" (González de Holguín 16, 338), or the "star of bad omens" (Rowe 1963, 304).

32. The Mexican nun Sor Juana Inés de la Cruz (1651–95) disguised one of the servants from her play *Los empeños de una casa* [*The Travails of a Home*] as a woman. In this play the servant pokes fun at the protagonist thus parodying amorous relations between the sexes (see Chang-Rodríguez 1978).

33. Let us remember that two women are responsible for the Israelite victory: Débora plans the strategy to defeat the Canaanite army, while Jael kills Sísara thus fulfilling the prophecy (II, ix, p. 286).

34. About female protagonists in colonial theater see Arrom (1978).

35. For a closer review of this attitude, see Chang-Rodríguez (1988, 58–62).

Chapter 5. Trespassing on Tradition: Francisco del Castillo's *La conquista del Perú*

1. It appeared in *Revista de Lima*, and was later published in *Tradiciones peruanas completas* (603–8). With regard to the nickname, it is generally accepted that del Castillo lost his eyesight before learning how to read. However, Ignacio de

Castro [anagram of Acignio Sartoc], a contemporary of his, proposed in an article dated 1791 that the author was not blind but nearsighted.

2. They are, "Un calembourg" ["A Calembourg"] (29–31) y "Otra improvisación del Ciego de la Merced" ["Another Improvisation by the Blind Poet from the Mercedarian Order"] (32).

3. The *Entremés del Justicia y litigantes* [*Interlude on Justice and the Plaintiffs*] ([1943] 1974, 262–75) was first published in his *De nuestro antiguo teatro* [*About Our Old Plays*]. Vargas Ugarte collected and edited several of del Castillo's dramatic short works: *Entremés del Viejo niño* [*The Interlude of the Old Child*], *Sainete, Fin de fiesta* or one-act play [*End of Presentation*], a *Loa* or prologue for the play *La conquista del Perú* [*The Conquest of Peru*] and *Mitrídates, rey del Ponto* [*Mithridates, King of the Pontus*] ([1943] 1974, 195–299).

4. See his *El arte dramático en Lima durante el virreinato* (1945, 413–25).

5. These plays can be found in manuscripts in three different libraries: 1) Archivo Histórico Nacional de Santiago de Chile, Fondo Antiguo, volume 6, under the title *Obras literarias de Fr. Francisco del Castillo* [*Literary Works by Fr. Francisco del Castillo*]; 2) National Library in Madrid (shelfmark 16.283), with the description *Comedias varias que ha compuesto el P. Fray Francisco del Castillo . . . 1749* [*Various Plays Composed by F. Fray Francisco del Castillo . . . 1749*]; and 3) Archivo General de la Nación de Buenos Aires, legajo Biblioteca Nacional 257, document 3666. See Reverte Bernal (1985a, 13).

6. In his doctoral dissertation Milla Batres transcribed the religious play *Guerra es la vida del hombre*, from the Madrid manuscript (see Reverte Bernal 1985a, 171–79).

7. See Arrom (1967, 108–9) and Reverte Bernal (1985a, 186–95).

8. Located in the cited manuscript from the Biblioteca Nacional in Madrid. I am grateful to Concepción Reverte Bernal for sending me the typescript of her edition of this work. Citations have been taken from that typescript; the folios corresponding to the Madrid manuscript have been indicated after each quote.

9. For the impact and circulation of this chronicle during the eighteenth century see Durand (1974) and Guibovich (1992).

10. In this regard, it is worth remembering that del Castillo in a poem lamented the devastation that the earthquake of 1747 caused in his "dulce patria" ["sweet fatherland"] (in Reedy, 52).

11. The Venezuelan Francisco de Miranda (1750–1816) proposed the restoration of the Tahuantinsuyu in an independent Spanish America.

12. For the causes of these changes see Lucena Samoral (27–33) and Franco (50–53).

13. See Reedy's comment about the romance "Conversación de dos escribanos receptores" ["Conversation between Two Scribes"] and "Conversación de un Negro, mayordomo de chacra con un Indio Alcalde de los Camarones, en la Calle de los Borricos" ["Conversation between a Black, Overseer of a Farm, with an Indian Mayor of Shrimp, on the Street of Borricos"] and "Declamación de un Filósofo contra la esclavitud perpetua de los negros, celoso de la libertad y respuesta de un mulato arpista en abono de la esclavitud" ["Declamation of a Philosopher Against the Perpetual Slavery of Blacks, Jealous for Liberty and Answer of a Mulatto Harpist in Favor of Slavery"] (46–49). The irony is that the philosopher argues in favor of freedom for the slaves, while the mulatto voices freedom's negative consequences for all, including slaves. With regard to del Castillo's conservative attitude see Reverte Bernal 1997, and Flores Galindo 1984.

14. The prestige of Inca royalty did not prevent del Castillo from writing a

long poem lauding the colonial administrators who, in 1750, defeated the rebellious Indians of Huarochirí. Nevertheless, the historic episode lacked the heroic character that the poet used to describe this event (see Reedy 1987).

15. One of them (c. 1724–28) whose intellectual author was Alonso de la Cueva (1684–1754), drew with obvious political motives the lords of Tahuantinsuyu followed by the Spanish kings; another, by José Palomino, was well known as it was included in *Viaje a la América Meridional* [*A Trip to South America*] (1748) by Jorge Juan and Antonio de Ulloa (Gisbert 1980, 128–32).

16. See Inca Garcilaso, second part of *Comentarios Reales* [*Royal Commentaries*], also known as *Historia general del Perú* [*General History of Peru*] bk. 1, chs. 12–13.

17. According to Lockhart (1986, 1:143), the animals were a puma and a jaguar; Candía fired his harquebus and the animals ran away.

18. See for example the comments of Espinosa Medrano to his reader ("Al letor"), ([1662] 1997, 41).

19. Among them were ineffective cannons used by Almagro el Mozo in the battle of Chupas (1542). Since the rebel believed that he had been betrayed by the Greek artilleryman, he killed him.

20. For the origin of these perceptions and how they were utilized by the conquistadors to subjugate the Indians, see Pease (1989b).

21. Reworked in a different fashion, the same argument was used by the Indigenous chronicler Felipe Guaman Poma de Ayala in *Primer nueva corónica y buen gobierno* [*First New Chronicle and Good Government*] (1615), to question the harsh actions first of conquistadors and later of colonial bureaucrats. The idea is related to the theory of "traslatio imperio" which gives the Spanish king the right of dominion over the Inca empire and its subjects. On this topic, see David Brading.

22. This is one of Garcilaso's theses to explain the swift conquest of Peru. The lack of communication coupled with the bad intentions of the interpreter were also evident in *Tragedia del fin de Atahualpa* [*Tragedy of Atahualpa's Death*] (see chapter 1) and in "dances of the conquest" studied by Wachtel (1976). In the drama, del Castillo does not dwell on this linguistic gap.

23. Several chroniclers have indicated that until the events in Cajamarca there had been only minor skirmishes between Spaniards and Andeans. At the same time, the invaders were provided with food stored in Inca warehouses, and guides in order to continue their inspection of the empire (see Rostworoski, 174).

24. For an analysis of this *loa* see Chang-Rodríguez (1996).

25. See in this regard the Mexican savant Carlos de Sigüenza y Góngora's *Alboroto y motín de los indios de México del 8 de junio de 1692*. About the complexities of criollo attitudes toward the indigenous population of Peru during the seventeenth century, see Mazzotti, and in the eighteenth century see Flores Galindo (1984).

26. Guaman Poma de Ayala centers his defense of the Andeans on this thesis (see his *Primer nueva corónica* [*First New Chronicle*] (1615) 1980, 1, 141 et passim).

27. According to this chronicler, Rumiñagüi "del pellexo [de Yllescas] hizo tanbor y de la cauesa hizo mate de ueuer chicha y de los güesos *antara* [flauta de Pan] y de los dientes y muelas *quiro guallca* [collar de dientes]" ["from Yllescas's skin he [Rumiñagüi] made a drum, and from his head he made a cup to drink chicha, and from the bones he made *antara* [flute] and from his teeth and molars *quiro guallca* [necklace]"] ([1615] 1980, 1:143).

28. The name comes from the Chilean epic poem *La Araucana* (1st part, 1568; 2nd part 1578; 3rd part 1589), by Alonso de Ercilla y Zúñiga (1533–1616). Guacolda or Huacolda is the wife of cacique Lautaro, an Indian lord who died defending his people (1, canto 13, 381–401).

Bibliography

Adorno, Rolena. "Arms, Letters and the Native Historian in Early Colonial Mexico." In *1492-1992: Re/Discovering Colonial Writing*, ed. René Jara and Nicholas Spadaccini, 201–24. Minneapolis: Prisma I, 1989.

———. *Cronista y Príncipe. La obra de don Felipe Guaman Poma de Ayala*. Lima: Pontificia Universidad Católica del Perú, 1989.

———. *Guaman Poma. Writing and Resistance in Colonial Peru*. Austin: University of Texas Press, 1986.

Allende, Isabel. "Ester Lucero." *Cuentos de Eva Luna*. Buenos Aires: Sudamericana, 1990. 121-29.

Aparicio, Severo. "Vida y obra poética del Ciego de la Merced de Lima." *Revista de Estudios de Madrid* 17.54 (1961): 457–79.

Arguedas, José María and Josafat Roel. "Puquio, una cultura en proceso de cambio." In *Formación de una cultura nacional indoamericana*, ed. Angel Rama, 34–79. Mexico: Siglo XXI, 1975.

Arrom, José J. "Cambiantes imágenes de la mujer en el teatro de la América virreinal." *Latin American Theatre Review* (1978): 5–15.

———. *Historia del teatro hispanoamericano (Epoca colonial)*. 2nd ed. Mexico: de Andrea, 1967.

———. *Imaginación del Nuevo Mundo*. Mexico: Siglo XXI, 1991.

———. "La Virgen del Cobre: historia, leyenda y símbolo sincrético." *Certidumbre de América*. 2nd ed. expanded. Madrid: Gredos, 1971. 184–214.

Arróniz, Othón. "Teatro misionero del siglo XVI." In *Historia de la literatura mexicana. Las literaturas amerindias de México y la literatura en español del siglo XVI*, ed. Beatriz Garza Cuarón and Georges Baudot, 388–415. Mexico: Siglo XXI, 1996.

Arzáns de Orsúa y Vela, Bartolomé. *Historia de la Villa Imperial de Potosí*. Ed. Lewis Hanke and Gunnar Mendoza. 3 vols. Providence: Brown University Press, 1965.

Balmori, Clemente Hernando. *La conquista de los españoles y el teatro indígena americano. Drama indígena bilingüe quechua castellano*. Ed. Ena Dargan. Trans., intro. and vocabulary by Clemente Hernando Balmori. Tucumán: Universidad Nacional de Tucumán, 1955.

———. "Introducción." In Balmori, 1955. 9–64.

Barreda Laos, Felipe. *Vida intelectual del Virreinato del Perú*. Buenos Aires: Talleres Gráficos Argentinos L. J. Rosso, 1937.

Berceo, Gonzalo de. *Los milagros de Nuestra Señora*. In *Obras completas*, vol. 2. Ed. Brian Dutton. London: Tamesis, 1971.

Bernales Ballesteros, Jorge. "La pintura en Lima durante el Virreinato." In *Pintura en el Virreinato del Perú*, 31–107. Lima: Banco de Crédito, 1989.

Beverley, John. "Nuevas vacilaciones sobre el barroco." *Revista de Crítica Literaria Latinoamericana* 28 (1988): 215–27.

Beyersdorff, Margot. *La adoración de los Reyes Magos*, vigencia del teatro religioso español en el Perú andino." Cuzco: Centro de Estudios Rurales Andinos "Bartolomé de las Casas," 1988.

———. "La 'puesta en texto' del primer drama indohispano en los Andes." *Revista de Crítica Literaria Latinoamericana* 37 (1993): 195–221.

Bhabha, Homi K. "Signs Taken for Wonders: Questions of Ambivalence and Authority under a Tree Outside Delhi, May 1817." In Gates, 1986. 163–84.

Bowers, Fredson. "Textual Introduction." Christopher Marlowe. *Doctor Faustus. The Complete Works of Christopher Marlowe.* Vol. 2. Ed. Fredson Bowers. 2nd ed. New York: Cambridge University Press, 1981. 123–59.

Brading, David A. *The First America. The Spanish Monarchy, Creole Patriots, and the Liberal State 1492–1867.* Cambridge: Cambridge University Press, 1991.

Burga, Manuel. *Nacimiento de una utopía: muerte y resurrección de los Incas.* Lima: Instituto de Apoyo Agrario, 1988.

Burkhart, Louise M. "The Voyage of Saint Amaro: A Spanish Legend in Nahuatl Literature." *Colonial Latin American Review* 4.1 (1995): 28–57.

Busto, José Antonio del. *José Gabriel Tupac Amaru antes de su rebelión.* Lima: Pontificia Universidad Católica del Perú, 1981.

Cárdenas, Gabriel de [Andrés González de Barcia]. "Prólogo." *Primera parte de los Comentarios Reales.* Madrid: Oficina real y a costa de Nicolás Rodríguez Franco, 1723. ix–xxxii.

Castillo, Francisco del. *El teatro de Fr. Francisco del Castillo ("el Ciego de la Merced").* Ed. Concepción Reverte Bernal. Barcelona: ETD-Micropublicaciones, 1988. (Biblioteca del Hispanista).

———. *Obra dramática.* Ed., intro. and notes by Concepción Reverte Bernal. In press [Presented as a doctoral thesis at the Universidad de Navarra, Pamplona, 1983].

———. *Obras.* Ed., intro. and notes by Rubén Vargas Ugarte, S. J. Lima: Studium, 1948.

Castro-Klarén, Sara. "Discurso y transformación de los dioses en los Andes: del Taki Onqoy a 'Rasu Ñiti.' " In Millones, 1990. 407–23.

———. "El siglo XVIII: sujetos sub-alternos y el teatro de la Perricholi." In *Mujer y cultura en la colonia hispanoamericana*, ed. Mabel Moraña, 295–306. Pittsburgh: Biblioteca de América, 1996.

Chang-Rodríguez, Raquel. *El discurso disidente. Ensayos de literatura colonial peruana.* Lima: Pontificia Universidad Católica del Perú, 1991.

———. *La apropiación del signo: tres cronistas indígenas del Perú.* Tempe: Center for Latin American Studies, Arizona State University, 1988.

———. "La princesa incaica Beatriz Clara y el dramaturgo ilustrado Francisco del Castillo." In *Mujer y cultura en la colonia hispanoamericana*, ed. Mabel Moraña, 51–66. Pittsburgh: Biblioteca de América, 1996.

———. "Relectura de *Los empeños de una casa.*" *Revista Iberoamericana* 44 (1978): 409–19. Synthesized en Cedomil Goic, *Historia y crítica de la literatura hispanoamericana.* Barcelona: Crítica, 1988. 365–68.

Cirlot, J. E. *A Dictionary of Symbols.* Trans. Jack Sage. 2nd ed. New York: Philosophical Society, 1981.

Cisneros, Luis Jaime. "Espinosa Medrano, *lectio aenigmatica.*" In *Diglosia linguo literaria y educación en el Perú,* ed. Enrique Ballón Aguirre and Rodolfo Cerrón Palomino, 243–51. Lima: 1989.

———. "Juan de Espinosa Medrano." In *Diccionario enciclopédico de las letras de América Latina* [DELAL], ed. José Ramón Medina, Nelson Osorio et al., 1674–80. Caracas: Biblioteca Ayacucho-Monte Avila, 1995.

———. "Rasgos de oralidad en el *Apologético* de Espinosa Medrano." In *Libro de Homenaje a Aurelio Miró Quesada,* 1:289–97. Lima: P. L. Villanueva, 1987.

———. "Sobre Espinosa Medrano: predicador, músico y poeta." *Cielo Abierto* 10.28 (1984): 3–8.

——— and Pedro Guibovich. "Juan de Espinosa Medrano, un intelectual cuzqueño del seiscientos: nuevos datos biográficos." *Revista de Indias* 48.182–83 (1988): 327–47.

———. "Un raro opúsculo del Lunarejo." *Lexis* 13.1 (1989): 95–115.

———. "Una biblioteca cuzqueña del siglo XVII." *Histórica* 6.2 (1982): 141–71.

Classen, Constance. *Inca Cosmology and the Human Body.* Salt Lake City: University of Utah Press, 1993.

Cornejo Polar, Antonio. *Escribir en el aire. Ensayo sobre la heterogeneidad sociocultural en las literaturas andinas.* Lima: Horizonte, 1994.

Cortés, Hernán. *Cartas de relación.* Ed. Angel Delgado Gómez. Madrid: Castalia, 1993.

Cosio, José Gabriel. "Los dramas quechuas *Usca Pauccar.*" *Revista Universitaria* (Organo de la Universidad del Cuzco). Año 5.17 (1916): 2–9.

Covarrubias, Sebastián de. *Tesoro de la Lengua Castellana o Española* [1611]. Madrid: Turner, n. d.

Del Busto, José Antonio. *José Gabriel Tupac Amaru antes de su rebelión.* Lima: Pontificia Universidad Católica del Perú, 1981.

Duncan, Barbara. "Statue Paintings of the Virgin." In *Gloria in Excelsis,* 1986. 32–57.

Durand, José. "El influjo de Garcilaso Inca en Tupac Amaru." *Realidad nacional.* Ed. and notes by Julio Ortega. Lima: Retablo de Papel, 1974. 208–15.

Duviols, Pierre. *Las destrucciones de las religiones andinas (conquista y colonia)* [1971]. Trans. Albor Maruenda. Mexico: UNAM, 1977.

El día de Lima [anónimo]. Lima, 1748.

Ercilla y Zúñiga, Alonso de. *La Araucana.* Ed., intro. and notes by Marcos A. Morínigo and Isaías Lerner. 2 vols. Madrid: Castalia, 1983.

Espinosa Medrano, Juan de [el Lunarejo]. *Apologético.* Ed., prologue and chronology by Augusto Tamayo Vargas. Caracas: Biblioteca Ayacucho, 1982.

———. *Apologético.* Ed. José Carlos González Boixo. Rome: Bulzoni, 1997.

———. *La novena maravilla.* Valladolid: Imprenta de Joseph de Rueda, 1695.

Espinoza Soriano, Waldemar. "Un movimiento religioso de libertad y salvación nativista. Yanahura-1596." In Ossio, 1973. 143–52.

Esquivel y Navia, Diego de. *Noticias cronológicas de la gran ciudad del Cuzco.* Ed., prologue and notes by Félix Denegri Luna with the collaboration of Horacio

Villanueva Urteaga and César Gutiérrez Muñoz. 2 vols. Lima: Banco Wiese Ltdo.-P. L. Villanueva, 1980.

Estabridis, Ricardo. *El grabado virreinal peruano.* Suelto. Lima: Banco Continental, 1987.

Flores Galindo, Alberto. *Aristocracia y plebe. Lima, 1760–1830 (Estructura de clase y sociedad colonial).* Lima: Mosca Azul, 1984.

———. *Buscando un inca: identidad y utopía en los Andes.* Lima: Instituto de Apoyo Agrario, 1987.

Franco, Jean. "La cultura hispanoamericana en la época colonial." In Iñigo Madrigal, 1982. 1:35–53.

Frank, Grace. "Introduction." Rutebeuf. *Le Miracle de Théophile.* 2nd ed. Paris, 1949.

Garcilaso de la Vega, el Inca. *Comentarios Reales.* Ed. Angel Rosenblat. Prologue by Ricardo Rojas. 2 vols. Buenos Aires: Emecé, 1943.

———. *Historia general del Perú* (Second part of *Comentarios Reales de los Incas*). Ed. Angel Rosenblat. Study of the second part of the *Comentarios Reales* by José de la Riva Agüero. 3 vols. Buenos Aires: Emecé, 1944.

Garibay K., Angel María. *Historia de la literatura náhuatl.* 2 vols. Mexico: Porrúa, 1953.

Gates, Henry Louis Jr., ed. *"Race," Writing and Difference.* Chicago: The University of Chicago Press, 1986.

Gisbert Mesa, Teresa. *Iconografía y mitos indígenas en el arte.* La Paz: Gisbert y Cía. S. A., 1980.

———. "Andean Painting." In *Gloria in Excelsis,* 1986a. 22–31.

———. "The Angels." In *Gloria in Excelsis,* 1986b. 58–63.

———. *Teatro virrenal en Bolivia.* La Paz: Biblioteca de Arte y Cultura Boliviana, 1962.

Gloria in Excelsis. The Virgin and Angels in Viceregal Painting of Peru and Bolivia. Guest Curators Barbara Duncan and Teresa Gisbert. New York: Center for Inter-American Relations, 1986.

Glantz, Margo. *Borrones y borradores.* Mexico: UNAM, 1992.

Glass, John B. "A Census of Middle American Testerian manuscripts." In *Handbook of Middle American Indians,* 14:281–961. Austin: University of Texas Press, 1975.

Gonzalbo Aizpuru, Pilar. *Historia de la educación en la época colonial. El mundo indígena.* Mexico: El Colegio de México, 1990.

González de Barcia, Andrés. See Cárdenas, Gabriel de.

González Boixo, José Carlos. "Introducción." In Espinosa Medrano, *Apologético,* 1997. 9–28.

González de Holguín, Diego. *Vocabulario de la lengua general de todo el Perú* [1608]. Prologue by Raúl Porras Barrenechea. Lima: UNMSM, 1952.

González Echevarría, Roberto. "Poetics and Modernity in Juan de Espinosa Medrano, Known as Lunarejo." In *Celestina's Brood. Continuities of the Baroque in Spanish and Latin American Literatures,* 149–69. Durham: Duke University Press, 1993.

Greenblatt, Stephen, ed. *New World Encounters.* Los Angeles: University of California Press, 1993.

Greenblatt, Stephen J. *Sir Walter Ralegh. The Renaissance Man and His Roles.* New Haven: Yale University Press, 1973.

Guaman Poma de Ayala, Felipe. *Primer nueva corónica y buen gobierno.* Ed. John V. Murra and Rolena Adorno. Trans. and textual analysis of Quechua by Jorge L. Urioste. 3 vols. Mexico: Siglo XXI, 1980.

Guibovich Pérez, Pedro. "Biobibliografía de Juan de Espinosa Medrano." *Boletín del Instituto Riva-Agüero* 15.122 (1988): 43–53.

———. "El testamento e inventario de bienes de Espinosa Medrano." *Histórica* 16.1 (1992): 1–31.

———. "Lectura y difusión de la obra de Garcilaso en el virreinato peruano (siglos XVII–XVIII). El caso de los *Comentarios Reales*." *Revista Histórica* 37 (1992): 103–20.

Gutiérrez, Gustavo. *Dios o el oro en las Indias (siglo XVI).* Lima: Instituto Bartolomé de las Casas, 1989.

Hampe Martínez, Teodoro. "La biblioteca del arzobispo Hernando Arias de Ugarte: bagaje intelectual de un prelado criollo (1614)." *Thesaurus* 40.2 (1987): 336–61.

Hanke, Lewis. "Viceroy Francisco de Toledo and the Just Titles of Spain to the Inca Empire." *The Americas* 3.1 (1946): 3–19.

Harris, Max. "The Dramatic Testimony of Antonio de Ciudad Real: Indigenous Theatre in Sixteenth-Century New Spain." *Colonial Latin American Review* 5.2 (1996): 237–51.

Harrison, Regina. *Signs, Songs and Memory in the Andes. Translating Quechua Language and Culture.* Austin: University of Texas Press, 1989.

Herzberg, Julia P. "Angels with Guns. Image and Interpretation." In *Gloria in Excelsis,* 1986. 64-75.

Hesse, Everett W. "Calderón's Popularity in the Spanish Indies." *Hispanic Review* 6 (1938): 277-93.

Hopkins Rodríguez, Eduardo. "Poética de Juan de Espinosa Medrano en el *Apologético en favor de D. Luis de Góngora*." *Revista de Crítica Literaria Latinoamericana* 78 (1978): 105–18.

Horcasitas, Fernando. *El teatro náhuatl: épocas novohispanas y moderna.* Mexico: UNAM, 1974.

Iñigo Madrigal, Luis, comp. *Historia de la literatura hispanoamericana. Epoca colonial.* Madrid: Cátedra, 1982.

Iriarte B., Francisco, et al. ed. *Dramas coloniales en el Perú actual.* Lima: Universidad Inca Garcilaso de la Vega, 1985.

Isbell, Billie Jean. "La otra mitad esencial: un estudio de complementariedad sexual andina." *Estudios Andinos* 5.1 (1976): 37–56.

Itier, César. *El teatro quechua en el Cuzco. Dramas y comedias de Nemesio Zúñiga Cazorla.* Lima: Institut Français d'Etudes Andines-Centro de Estudios Regionales Andinos "Bartolomé de las Casas," 1995.

Johnson, Julie Greer. *Satire in Colonial Spanish America. Turning the New World Upside Down.* Austin: University of Texas Press, 1993.

Kapsoli, Wilfredo. "La muerte del rey Inca en las danzas populares y la relación de Pomabamba." *Tierradentro* 3 (1985): 157–74.

Karttunen, Frances. *Between Worlds. Interpreters, Guides and Survivors.* New Brunswick, N.J.: Rutgers University Press, 1994.

Klor de Alva, Jorge. "El discurso nahua y la apropiación de lo europeo." In *De palabra y obra en el Nuevo Mundo. Imágenes interétnicas*, ed. Miguel León Portilla et al. Mexico: Siglo XXI, 1992. 339–68.

Kozinska Frybes, Joanna. "La representación encarnada: una reflexión sobre el teatro evangelizador en Nueva España." *Foro Hispánico* 4 (1992): 101–13.

Lara, Jesús. *La literatura de los quechuas. Ensayo y antología*. Cochabamba: Canelas, 1960.

———, ed., trans. and intro. *Tragedia del fin de Atau Wallpa*. Cochabamba: Imprenta Universitaria, 1957.

Leonard, Irving A. *Books of the Brave*. Ed. and intro. Rolena Adorno. Berkeley: University of California Press, 1992.

———. "El teatro en Lima, 1790–93." *Hispanic Review* 8 (1940): 93–112.

———. "Notes on Lope de Vega's Works in the Spanish Indies." *Hispanic Review* 6 (1938): 277-93.

Levillier, Roberto. *Don Francisco de Toledo, supremo organizador del Perú. Su vida, su obra (1515–1582)*. Madrid: Espasa-Calpe, 1935.

Lienhard, Martin. *La voz y su huella. Escritura y conflicto étnico-social en América Latina 1492–1988*. Hanover, NH: Ediciones del Norte, 1991.

Loayza, Francisco. *Juan Santos, el invencible*. Lima, 1942.

Loayza, Luis. *El sol de Lima*. Lima: Mosca Azul, 1974.

Lockhart, James. *Los de Cajamarca. Un estudio social y biográfico de los primeros conquistadores del Perú* [1972]. Trans. Mariana Mould de Pease. 2 vols. Lima: Milla Batres, 1986.

———. *The Nahuas after the Conquest: A Social and Cultural History of the Indians of Central Mexico. Sixteenth through Eighteenth Centuries*. Stanford: Stanford University Press, 1992.

———. *Nahuas and Spaniards: Postconquest Central Mexican History and Philology*. Stanford: Stanford University Press, 1991.

———and Stuart B. Schwartz. *Early Latin America. A History of Colonial Spanish America and Brazil*. New York: Cambridge University Press, 1983.

Lohmann Villena, Guillermo. *El arte dramático en Lima durante el virreinato*. Madrid: CSIC, 1945.

———. *Las minas de Huancavelica en los siglos XVI y XVII*. Sevilla: Escuela de Estudios Hispano-Americanos, 1949.

———, ed. *Un tríptico del Perú virrenal: el Virrey Amat, el Marqués de Soto Florido y La Perricholi*. North Carolina Studies in the Romance Languages and Literatures, 15. Chapel Hill: University of North Carolina, 1976.

———and Raúl Moglia. "Repertorio de las representaciones teatrales en Lima hasta el siglo XVIII." *Revista de Filología Hispánica* 5 (1943): 313–43.

López Baralt, Mercedes. *El retorno del Inca rey: mito y profecía en el mundo andino*. Madrid: Playor, 1987.

———. *Icono y conquista: Guamán Poma de Ayala*. Madrid: Hiperión, 1988.

Lucena Samoral, Manuel. "Hispanoamérica en la época colonial." In Iñigo Madrigal, 1982. 1:11-33.

Luciani, Frederick. "Spanish American Theatre of the Colonial Period." In *The Cambridge History of Latin American Literature*, ed. Roberto González Echevarría and Enrique Pupo-Walker, 1:260–85. Cambridge: Cambridge University Press, 1994.

———. "Spanish American Theatre in the Eighteenth Century." In *The Cambridge History of Latin American Literature*, ed. Roberto González Echevarría and Enrique Pupo-Walker, 1:401–16. Cambridge: Cambridge University Press, 1993.

Ludmer, Josefina. "Las tretas del débil." In *La sartén por el mango*, ed. Patricia Elena González and Eliana Ortega, 47–54. San Juan, Puerto Rico: Huracán, 1985.

MacCormack, Sabine. *Religion in the Andes. Vision and Imagination in Early Colonial Peru*. Princeton: Princeton University Press, 1991.

Mannheim, Bruce. "On the Sibilants of Colonial Southern Peruvian Quechua." *International Journal of American Linguistics* 54.2 (1988): 168–208.

Martín, Luis. *The Intellectual Conquest of Peru*. New York: Fordham University Press, 1968.

Matto de Turner, Clorinda. *Don Juan de Espinosa Medrano o sea el doctor Lunarejo*. Lima: Imprenta del Universo de Carlos Prince, 1887.

———. *Bocetos a lápiz de americanos célebres*. Lima: Bacigalupi, 1890.

Mazzotti, José Antonio. "La heterogeneidad colonial peruana y la construcción del discurso criollo en el siglo XVII." In *Asedios a la heterogeneidad cultural. Libro de homenaje a Antonio Cornejo Polar*, ed. José Antonio Mazzotti and U. Juan Zevallos Aguilar, 173–96. Philadelphia: Asociación Internacional de Peruanistas, 1996.

Meneses, Teodoro L. "El *Usca Paucar* drama religioso en quechua del siglo XVIII." *Documenta* 2.1 (1949–50): 1–178.

———. "Cuatricentenario de la cátedra de quechua en San Marcos." In *Aula Quechua*, comp. Rodolfo Cerrón Palomino, 237–46. Lima: Signo, 1982.

———. *Teatro quechua colonial. Antología*. Lima: Edubanco, 1983.

———, ed., trans. and intro. *La muerte de Atahualpa, drama quechua de autor anónimo*. Lima: UNMSM, 1987.

Mesa, José de and Teresa Gisbert. *Historia de la pintura cuzqueña*. Buenos Aires: Universidad de Buenos Aires-Facultad de Arquitectura y Urbanismo, 1962.

———. *Holguín y la pintura virreinal peruana*. La Paz: Juventud, 1977.

Middendorf, E. W. *Dramatische und Lyrische Dichtungen der Keshua Sprache*. Leipzig, 1891.

Mignolo, Walter. "Anáhuac y sus otros: la cuestión de la letra en el Nuevo Mundo." *Revista de Crítica Literaria Latinoamericana* 28 (1988): 29–54.

———. "Semiosis colonial: la dialéctica entre representaciones fracturadas y hermenéuticas pluritópicas." *Foro Hispánico* 4 (1992): 11–27.

Milla Batres, Carlos, ed. *Diccionario histórico y biográfico del Perú*. 9 vols. Lima: Milla Batres, 1986.

———. "Vida y obra literaria édita e inédita del Ciego de la Merced: Fray Francisco del Castillo Andraca y Tamayo (1716–1770)." PhD. dissertation. Lima, UNMSM, 1976.

Millones, Luis. *Actores de altura. Ensayos sobre el teatro popular andino*. Lima: Horizonte, 1992.

———. *El Inca por la Coya. Historia de un drama popular en los Andes peruanos.* Lima: Fundación Friedrich Ebert, 1988.

———. *Historia y poder en los Andes centrales.* Madrid: Alianza, 1987.

———. "Taki Onqoy." *Cielo Abierto* 10.28 (1984): 9–15.

———, comp. *El retorno de las huacas. Estudios y documentos sobre el Taki Onqoy. Siglo XVI.* Lima: IEP-SPP, 1990.

Mills, Kenneth. "Bad Christians in Colonial Peru." *Colonial Latin American Review* 5.2 (1996): 183–218.

Miró Quesada, Aurelio. "Prólogo." In *Comentarios Reales de los incas.* Lima: Banco de Crédito del Perú, 1985. xiii–xlvi.

Montoya, Rodrigo. *La cultura quechua hoy.* Lima: Mosca Azul, 1987.

Moraña, Mabel. "Barroco y conciencia criolla en Hispanoamérica." *Revista de Crítica Literaria Latinoamericana* 28 (1988): 229–51.

———, ed. *Relecturas del barroco de Indias.* Hanover, N.H.: Ediciones del Norte, 1994.

Mörner, Magnus. *Actividades políticas y económicas de los jesuitas en el Río de La Plata.* Buenos Aires, 1968.

Mujica Pinilla, Ramón. "Los ángeles de la conquista y las plumas del sol." *Revista de Estudios Hispánicos* (Special Issue, 1992): 309–19.

The New Oxford Annotated Bible (Revised Standard Version). Ed. Herbert G. May and Bruce M. Metzger. New York: Oxford University Press, 1977.

Núñez Cáceres, Javier. "La primera edición del *Apologético* de Espinosa Medrano." *El Cuervo* (Aguadilla, Puerto Rico) 1 (1989): 72–75.

———. "Propósito y originalidad del *Apologético* de Juan de Espinosa Medrano." *Nueva Revista de Filología Hispánica* 32 (1983): 170–75.

Ocaña, Diego de. *Comedia de Nuestra Señora de Guadalupe y sus milagros* [1601]. Preliminary study and notes by Teresa Gisbert. La Paz: Biblioteca Paceña, 1957.

O'Phelan, Scarlett. *Rebellions and Revolts in Eighteenth Century Peru and Upper Peru.* Cologne: Böhlau Verlag, 1985.

Ossio, Juan M., ed. *Ideología mesiánica del mundo andino.* Lima: Ignacio Prado Pastor, 1973.

———. "Introducción." In Ossio, 1973. xi–xlv.

Pagden, Anthony. *The Fall of Natural Man: The American Indian and the Origins of Comparative Ethnology.* Cambridge: Cambridge University Press, 1982.

Palma, Ricardo. *Tradiciones en salsa verde.* Ed. and prologue by Francisco Carrillo and Carlos Garayar. 2nd ed. Lima: Biblioteca Universitaria, 1973.

———. *Tradiciones peruanas completas.* Ed. and prologue by Edith Palma. Madrid: Aguilar, 1957.

Pareja, Francisco de. *Doctrina cristiana muy útil y necesaria.* Mexico, 1578. Ed. Luis Resines. Salamanca: Ediciones de la Universidad de Salamanca, 1990.

París, Marta de. "El teatro y los indios en el área de influencia guaranítica." *Latin American Theatre Review* 21.1 (1987): 95–98.

Parker, Alexander A. "The Approach to the Spanish Drama of the Golden Age" [1957]. *Diamante Series.* London: The Hispanic and Luso-Brazilian Councils, 1964.

Pease G. Y., Franklin. "Continuidad y resistencia de lo andino." *Allpanchis Phuturinqa* 17–18 (1981): 105–18.

———. *Del Tawantinsuyu a la historia del Perú*. 2nd ed. Lima: Pontificia Universidad Católica del Perú, 1989a.

———. "El mito de Inkarrí y la visión de los vencidos." In Ossio, 1973. 441–55.

———. "La conquista española y la percepción andina del otro." *Histórica* 13.2 (1989b): 171–96.

———. *Las crónicas y los Andes*. Lima: Pontificia Universidad Católica del Perú-Fondo de Cultura Económica, 1995.

———. *Los últimos incas del Cuzco*. 2nd ed. Lima: P. L. Villanueva, 1976.

———. "Mesianismo andino e identidad étnica: continuidades y problemas." *Cultura* (Ecuador) 5.13 (1982): 57–71.

———, ed., prologue and bibliography. *El pensamiento mítico*. Lima: Mosca Azul, 1982. 9–28.

Porras Barrenechea, Raúl. "Prólogo." In González de Holguín, 1952. v–xliv.

Raleigh, Sir Walter. *The Discovery of Guiana*. In *Works*, ed. Oldys and Birch, 8:391–476. New York: Burt Franklin, n. d.

Rama, Angel. *La ciudad letrada*. Hanover, N.H.: Ediciones del Norte, 1984.

Ramos Gavilán, Alonso. *Historia de nuestra Señora de Copacabana* [1621]. 2nd ed. La Paz: Academia Boliviana de la Historia-Editora Universo, 1976.

Ravicz, Marilyn Ekdahl. *Early Colonial Religious Drama in Mexico. From Zompantli to Golgotha*. Washington D.C.: Catholic University of America, 1970.

Reedy, Daniel R. "El Ciego de la Merced: A Blind Poet's View of Popular Culture in Eighteenth-Century Lima." In *Retrospect: Essays on Latin American Literature (In Memory of Willis Knapp Jones)*, ed. Elizabeth S. Rogers and Timothy J. Rogers, 40–54. York: Spanish Literature Publications Co., 1987.

Resines Llorente, Luis. *Catecismos americanos del siglo XVI*. Vol. 1. Valladolid: Junta de Castilla y León, 1992.

Reverte Bernal, Concepción. *Aproximación crítica a un dramaturgo virreinal peruano: Fr. Francisco del Castillo ("El Ciego de la Merced")*. Cádiz: Servicio de Publicaciones de la Universidad de Cádiz, 1985a.

———. "Guía bibliográfica para el estudio del teatro virrenal peruano." *Historiografía y Bibliografía Americanista* 29 (1985b): 129–50.

———. "Hacia un corpus completo de las obras de Fr. Francisco del Castillo" (Lima, 1716–1770). *Anales de Literatura Hispanoamericana* 20 (1991): 263–98.

———. "Notas para un estudio de la "Mise en scene" de una comedia histórica hispanoamericana: *La conquista del Perú*, de Fr. Francisco del Castillo (Lima, 1716–1770)." *Anales de Literatura Hispanoamericana* 12 (1983): 115–28.

———. "Saber teológico y moral en las obras de Fray Francisco del Castillo, 'el Ciego de la Merced'." In *Pensamiento europeo y cultura colonial*, ed. Karl Kohut and Sonia Rose, 137–62. Frankfurt am Main: Vervuert; Madrid: Iberoamericana, 1997.

———. "Un poeta virreinal peruano: Fray Francisco del Castillo, 'el Ciego de la Merced.' " *Estudios* (Mexico) 12 (1988): 69–88.

———, ed., intro. and notes. *Obra dramática* [of Francisco del Castillo]. In press [Presented as a doctoral thesis at the Universidad de Navarra, Pamplona, 1983].

Richards, Stanley. "Peter Shaffer." In *Best Plays of The Sixties*, ed. with an introductory note and prefaces to the plays by Stanley Richards, 523–26. Garden City: Doubleday and Co., 1970.

Rimac, Juan del [Rubén Vargas Ugarte]. "Una comedia inédita del Lunarejo." *Revista de la Universidad Católica del Perú* 1–5, 7–9 (1932–34): 36–44, 103–12, 181–92, 309–21, 403–14; 597–606, 20–27, 108–15.

Rodríguez Garrido, José A. "Aproximación a la oratoria sagrada de Espinosa Medrano." *Boletín del Instituto Riva-Agüero* 15.122 (1988): 11–32.

Roggiano, Alfredo A. "Juan de Espinosa Medrano: apertura hacia un espacio crítico en las letras de la América Latina." In *Prosa hispanoamericana virreinal*, ed. Raquel Chang-Rodríguez, 101–11. Barcelona: Hispam, 1978.

Rojas Garcidueñas, José. *El teatro de Nueva España en el siglo XVI* [1935]. Mexico: SepSetentas, 1973.

Rostworowski de Diez Canseco, María. *Historia del Tahuantinsuyu*. Lima: IEP, 1988.

Rowe, John H. "El movimiento nacional inca del siglo XVIII." *Revista Universitaria* (Cuzco) 43.107 (1954): 17–47.

―――. "Inca Culture at the Time of the Spanish Conquest." In *Handbook of South American Indians*, ed. Julian H. Steward, 2:183–330. New York: Cooper Square Publishers, 1963.

Said, Edward W. *Orientalism*. New York: Vintage Books, 1978.

Sartoc, Acignio [Ignacio de Castro]. "Disertación sobre la ceguedad ilustrada." *Mercurio Peruano* 57–58 (1791): 210–16, 218–25.

Scott, James C. *Domination and the Arts of Resistance*. New Haven: Yale University Press, 1990.

Shaffer, Peter. *The Royal Hunt of The Sun*. In *Best Plays of the Sixties*, ed. with an introductory note and prefaces to the plays by Stanley Richards, 531–622. Garden City: Doubleday and Co., 1970.

Shelley, Kathleen and Grínor Rojo. "El teatro hispanoamericano colonial." In Iñigo Madrigal, 1982. 1:319–52.

Sigüenza y Góngora, Carlos de. *Alboroto y motín de los indios de México del 8 de junio de 1692*. Ed. Irving A. Leonard. Mexico: Museo Nacional de Arqueología, Historia y Etnografía, 1932.

Souto Alabarce, Arturo. *Teatro indiano de los Siglos de Oro*. Mexico: Trillas, 1988.

Stern, Steve J. "The Age of Andean Insurrection, 1742–1782: A Reappraisal." In *Resistance, Rebellion, and Consciousness in the Andean Peasant World, 18th to 20th Centuries*, ed. Steve J. Stern, 34–93. Madison: University of Wisconsin Press, 1987.

Suárez-Radillo, Carlos Miguel. *El teatro barroco hispanoamericano: ensayo de una historia crítico-antológica*. 3 vols. Madrid: José Porrúa Turanzas, 1981.

―――. *El teatro clásico y costumbrista hispanoamericano: una historia crítico-antológica*. 2 vols. Madrid: Cultura Hispánica, 1984.

Szeminski, Jan. *La utopía tupamarista*. Lima: Pontificia Universidad Católica del Perú, 1983.

Tamayo Rodríguez, J. Agustín. *Estudios sobre Juan de Espinosa Medrano, "el Lunarejo."* Lima: Studium, 1971.

Tauro, Alberto, ed. *Enciclopedia ilustrada del Perú*. 7 vols. Lima: PEISA, 1987.

Temple, Ella Dunbar. "Un linaje incaico durante la dominación española. Los Sahuaraura." *Revista Histórica* 18 (1949): 70–77.

Terracini, Lore. "L'incomprensione linguistica nella Conquista spagnola; drama per i vinti, comicità per i vincitori." *I codici del silenzio.* Turin: Edizioni dell'Orso, 1988. 198–229.

Tibesar, Antonine. *Franciscan Beginnings in Colonial Peru.* Washington D. C.: Academy of American Franciscan History, 1953.

Titu Cusi Yupanqui, Diego de Castro. *Ynstruçión del Ynqa . . . [Relación de la conquista del Perú].* Ed. Luis Millones. Lima: El Virrey, 1985.

Tord, Luis Enrique. "La pintura virreinal en el Cusco." In *Pintura en el Virreinato del Perú,* 167-210. Lima: Banco de Crédito, 1989.

———. "The Viceroyalty of Peru, 1532–1825." In *Gloria in Excelsis,* 1986. 6–21.

Tragedia del fin de Atahualpa. In Meneses, 1983. 527–87.

Unzueta, Mario. *Valle.* Cochabamba, 1945.

Valbuena Briones, A. "Nota preliminar." Pedro Calderón de la Barca. *El mágico prodigioso.* In *Obras completas,* 1:603–8. Madrid: Aguilar, 1969.

Valbuena Prat, Angel. "Prólogo." In [Antonio] Mira de Amescua. *Teatro,* 1:ix-lxxviii. Madrid: Espasa-Calpe, 1960.

Valcárcel, Carlos Daniel. *Historia de la educación colonial.* Lima: Universo, 1968.

———. *La rebelión de Tupac Amaru.* Lima: PEISA, 1973.

———. *Rebeliones indígenas.* Lima: PTCM, 1946.

———. *Tupac Amaru, precursor de la independencia.* Lima: UNMSM, 1977.

Valcárcel, Luis E. "Noticia sobre un nuevo texto quechua del *Usca Paucar.*" *Actas y trabajos científicos del XXVII Congreso Internacional de Americanistas.* Vol. 2. Lima, 1942. 76–79.

Vargas Llosa, Mario. "El Lunarejo en Asturias." In *Libro de Homenaje a Aurelio Miró Quesada,* 2:893–97. Lima: P. L. Villanueva, 1987.

Vargas Ugarte, Rubén, S. J. *Concilios Limenses: 1551–1772.* 3 vols. Lima: Talleres Gráficos de la Tipografía Peruana, 1951–54.

———. *Historia de la Compañía de Jesús en el Perú.* Burgos: Aldecoa, 1963.

———. *Historia del culto de María en Iberoamérica y de sus imágenes y santuarios más celebrados.* 2nd ed. Buenos Aires: Huarpes, 1947.

———. *Los jesuitas del Perú y el arte.* Lima: Librería e Imprenta Gil, 1963.

———, ed., intro. and notes. *De nuestro antiguo teatro.* Lima: Compañía de Impresiones y Publicidad, 1943.

———, intro. and notes. *De nuestro antiguo teatro. Colección de piezas dramáticas de los siglos XVI, XVII y XVIII* [1943]. Lima: Milla Batres, 1974.

Varón Gabai, Rafael. "El Taki Onqoy: las raíces andinas de un fenómeno colonial." In Millones, 1990. 331–405.

Wachtel, Nathan. *Los vencidos. Los indios del Perú frente a la conquista española* [1971]. Trans. Antonio Escohotado. Madrid: Alianza, 1976.

Williams, Jerry M. *El teatro del México colonial. Epoca misionera.* New York: Peter Lang, 1992.

———. "The Sixteenth Century Mexican Stage: Authority and Conflict." *Revista de Estudios Hispánicos* 23.3 (1990): 21–35.

Zimmerman, Arthur F. *Francisco de Toledo. Fifth Viceroy of Peru 1569–1581* [1938]. New York: Greenwood, 1968.

———. *La Historia de la Villa Imperial de Potosí.* Lima: UNMSM, 1966.

Index

Albornoz, Cristóbal de, 48
Alboroto y motín de los indios de México del 8 de junio de 1692, 128n
Allende, Isabel, 59
Almagro, Diego de, 36, 41, 52–53
Almagro el Mozo, 128n
Alvarez, Arturo, 123n
Amar su propia muerte, 18, 83–84, 90, 92–94, 96–97, 118
Amaro (or Amalo), Saint, 25
Anson, George, Admiral, 120n
Aparicio, Severo, 16, 98
Apologético en favor de D. Luis de Góngora, Príncipe de los poetas líricos de España, 84–86, 88
Araucana, La, 128n
Arias de Ugarte, Hernando, bishop, 125n
Arguedas, José María, 43
Aristotle, 32
Arrom, José Juan, 16, 101, 111
Arzáns de Orsúa y Vela, Bartolomé, 49
Atahualpa, Incan king, 36, 39, 41, 43, 47, 49–56, 58, 93, 100–101, 108–14, 117, 119n, 121n, 122n
Atahualpa, Juan Santos, 38–39, 41, 43, 53
Atahualpa cycle. *See* conquest cycle
Atau Wallpaj P'uchukakuyninpa Wankan. See *Tragedia del fin de Atahualpa*
Augustinian Order, 32, 68, 86
Ayacucho, Battle of, 122n

Bacchus, 92
bailes [dances], 16
Barac, 90, 95
Barachiel, archangel, 124n
Bardiel, "angel of hail", 124n
Bato, 91–92
Benalcázar, Sebastián de, 114
Berceo, Gonzalo de, 59, 61

Berreo, Antonio de, Governor of Trinidad, 120n
Bitti, Bernardo, 63
Book of Judges, 95
Borja y Aragón, Francisco de, Príncipe de Esquilache, Viceroy of Peru, 89
Bry, Theodore de, 120n
Burkhart, Louise M., 25, 29
Busto, José Antonio del, 120n

Calcuchima, 52
Calderón de la Barca, Pedro, 59, 61, 90, 100
Cañari Indians, 114, 121n
Candelaria [Virgin of Candlemas], 68
Candía, Pedro de, "el griego" [the Greek], 100, 102, 104, 108, 128n
capullana [female rulers], 95
Cárdenas, Gabriel de, 40–41, 101, 120n
Castillo, Francisco del [Ciego de la Merced], 16, 18, 97–102, 104–5, 108–10, 114, 116, 118, 127n, 128n
Castro, Ignacio de, 124n, 126–27n
Catecismo de la doctrina cristiana, 31
Catholic kings, 30
Cay Pacha [place where humans and animals reside], 93
chala [dry stems from corn plants or paper], 53
champi [a mace], 80–81
Charles V, 24, 121n
Chi, Gaspar Antonio, 119n
Chocne, Juan, 48
Chupas, Battle of, 128n
Church of Saint Peter (Lima), 75
Ciego de la Merced. *See* Castillo, Francisco del
Cisneros, Luis Jaime, 85, 87, 124n, 125n
Clement X, Pope, 124n

Colegio de Santa Cruz de Tlatelolco, 30
Columbus, Christopher, 40–41
Comedia de Nuestra Señora de Guadalupe y sus milagros, 64
Comentarios Reales, 18, 33–34, 36, 40–41, 54, 56, 62, 97, 101, 104, 108, 109, 118, 120n, 128n
conquest cycle, 18, 36, 41, 47, 49–50, 53, 120n
conquista del Perú, La, 18, 99–102, 111–12, 113, 118, 127n; *loa*, 100, 111, 127n
Contreras y Valverde, Vasco Jacinto de, later Bishop of Popayán, 60, 122n
Copacabana, Virgin of, 68, 71, 124n; shrine of, 68
Cortés, Hernán, 24, 32
Cortéz de la Cruz, Antonio, 84–85, 125n
Council of Lima: First, 62; Second, 62; Third, 62, 68, 71
Council of Trent, 62–63
Counter-Reformation, 63, 75
Covarrubias, Sebastián de, 86, 92
Coya, Beatriz Clara, 111
coyas [Inca queens], 95
Cruz, Sor Juana Inés de la, 126n
Cueva, Alonso de la, 128n
Culiscacha, 100
curaca [Andean lord], 89

De nuestro antiguo teatro, 127n
Débora, 91, 94–96, 126n
Degollación de don Juan Atahualpa en Cajamarca (painting), 47
Devil, 59–61, 76, 80, 82–83, 124n
día de Lima, El, 100
Discoverie of the large and beautiful empire of Guiana, The, 41
Discurso [sobre si en un curso de opositores a beneficio . . .], 86–87, 124n
Doctor Faustus, 60, 122n
Doctrina cristiana en lengua mexicana, 25
Doctrina cristiana muy útil y necesaria, 25
Doctrina cristiana y catecismo para instrucción de indios, traducida en las dos lenguas generales destos reynos, quichua y aymara, 62
Dominican Order, 32, 36, 53, 68, 80, 84–85, 87, 89, 94, 96, 123n, 125n, 126n
Drake, Francis, 41

empeños de una casa, Los, 126n
Enoch, book of, 124n
Entremés del Justicia y litigantes, 127n
Entremés del Viejo niño, 127n
Ercilla y Zúñiga, Alonso de, 128n
esclavo del demonio, El, 59
Espinosa Medrano, Juan de, 18, 83–92, 94–97, 118, 122n, 124n, 125n, 126n, 128n
Esquivel y Navia, Diego de, 124n, 126n

Faria y Souza, Manuel de, 84
Faust, 60
Faust-Buch, 122n
Faust, Doctor, 60
Felipillo, 36, 50, 52–54
Fernando VI, 100, 108, 111, 116
"Fiesta de los naturales" [Indian Festivity], 100
Franciscan Order, 25, 30–32
Fuenteovejuna, 94

Gabriel, archangel, 75, 124n
Gante, Pedro de, 25, 31
García de Loyola, Martín, 111
Garcilaso de la Vega, Inca, 18, 33–34, 36, 40, 54, 56, 62, 68, 80, 97, 101, 105, 114, 118, 128n
Garibay, Angel María, 31
Gisbert, Teresa, 41, 75, 102, 123n
Goethe, 60
Góngora, Luis de, 84
González de Barcia, Andrés. *See* Cárdenas, Gabriel de
González de Holguín, Diego, 123n
González Echevarría, Roberto, 125n
Gramática de la lengua castellana, 30
Gramática o arte de la lengua general de los indios del Reyno del Perú, 123n
guacas [local gods], 48
Guacolda (or Huacolda), 128n
Guadalupe, Convent of (Extremadura), 64
Guadalupe, Virgin of, 64
Guaman Poma de Ayala, Felipe, 36,

41, 43, 56, 64, 68, 71, 80, 114, 126n, 128n
Guardian Angel, devotion to, 75, 124n
Guerra es la vida del hombre, 99, 127n
Guibovich, Pedro, 85, 87

Hanan Pacha [place where deities reside], 93
Heber Cineo, 90–92, 94–96
hijo pródigo, El, 84
Historia alegórica del Anticristo y el Juicio Final, 126n
Historia de la Villa Imperial de Potosí, 49
Historia general de las cosas de Nueva España, 119n
Huacolda, 100, 113–14
huaqaripuni [heroic deeds of Inca kings], 34
Huarochirí, 128n
Huascar, 93, 100–101, 108, 113, 121n
Huascar Inca, 120n
Huaylla Huisa, 50, 52
Huayna Capac, 93, 100, 104–5, 108–9, 113–14, 121n

Ignatius of Loyola, Saint, 125n
Inkarrí (or *Inca Rey*) [Inca King], 43, 54, 121n
Itier, César, 16

Jabín, king, 90–95
Jael, 90–91, 94–96, 126n
Jehudiel, archangel, 124n
Jesuit Order, 32, 34, 39, 75, 80, 85, 87, 89–90, 96, 120n, 123n, 125n, 126n
Jori Tica, 61, 71
Juan, Jorge, 128n

Klor de Alva, Jorge, 30

Landa, Diego de, later Bishop of Yucatan, 23, 119n
Lara, Jesús, 16, 38, 49
Lautaro, 128n
Lazarillo de Tormes, 81–82
Leonard, Irving A., 90
Lexicón o Vocabulario de la lengua general del Perú, 123n
Lezama Lima, José, 125n
Llupanguillo, 111
lógica, La, 85, 87

Lohmann Villena, Guillermo, 16, 98
López Baralt, Mercedes, 121n, 124n
Loyola y Vergara, Francisco de, 86
Luciani, Frederick, 16
Ludmer, Josefina, 126n
Lunarejo, El. *See* Espinosa Medrano, Juan de

mágico prodigioso, El, 59
mallqui [mummified bodies], 55, 122n
Mama Huaco, 95, 100, 113
Manco Capac, 121n
Manco Inca, 48, 53, 68, 80, 82, 96, 121n
Mannheim, Bruce, 60
Manso de Velasco, José, Count of Superunda, Viceroy of Peru, 100
Marian cult. *See* Virgin Mary, cult of
Marlowe, Christopher, 59–60, 122n
maskapaicha [royal emblem], 40
Matto de Turner, Clorinda, 85
Medoro, Angelino, 63
Meneses, Teodoro, 16, 60, 119n, 122n, 124n
Mercedarian Order, 18, 98–99, 127n
Michael, archangel, 75–76, 80, 124n
Middendorf, E. W., 60, 122n
Milagros de Nuestra Señora, 59
Milla Batres, Carlos, 16, 98, 127n
Mira de Amescua, Antonio, 59, 61
Miranda, Francisco de, 127n
mitayos [conscripted Indian loborers], 91
Mitrídates, rey del Ponto, 99, 127n
Montiel y Surco, Miguel, 40
Mosco, 91–92
Mulhmann, W., 48–49
muru onqoy [sickness of the spots], 121n

Nebrija, Antonio de, 30
Ni amor se libra de amor, 100
Ninan Cuyoche, 105
Nova typis transacta, navigatio, novi orbis, Indiae Occidentalis, 40
novena maravilla, La, 85, 87, 125n
Nuestra Señora de la Peña de Francia [Our Lady of the Rock of France], 71, 124n
Núñez de Balboa, Vasco, 41
ñustas [royal princesses], 52, 54

Ocaña, Jerónimo Diego de, 64
Ollantay, 120 n, 122 n
Oré, Luis Gerónimo de, 123 n
Oropesa, Marquis of. *See* Tupac Amaru II, José Gabriel Condorcanqui

pachacuti [cosmic cataclysm], 50, 93
Pachamama [Mother Earth], 68
Palma, Ricardo, 98–99
Palomino, José, 128 n
Panegírica declamación por la protección de las ciencias y estudios, 86
Pareja, Francisco de, 25
Paul V, Pope, 71, 123 n
Pease, Franklin, 38, 43, 52
Peralta Barnuevo Rocha y Benavides, Pedro de, 124 n
Pérez de Alesio, Mateo, 63
Perfecto de Salas, José, 99
Peter, Saint, 71
Philoponus, Honorius. *See* Plautius, Caspar
Phillip II, 56, 63
Pizarro, Francisco, 36, 41, 47–48, 50, 52–56, 58, 100–102, 108, 113, 121 n
Pizarro, Pedro, 121 n
Plautius, Caspar (Abbot of Seittenstetten), 40
Pliny, 86
pobre más rico, El, 60
Pomata, Virgin of, 68, 71, 80, 123–24 n; shrine of, 68, 123 n
Porras Barrenechea, Raúl, 88
Primer nueva corónica y buen gobierno, 36, 43, 56, 71, 120 n, 124 n, 128 n
Príncipe, school (Lima), 89
Psalmodia christiana y sermonario de los sanctos del año en lengua mexicana, 119 n
Pumacahua, Mateo, 122 n
puru qaylla [Ritual funerals of Inca lords], 34

Quespillo, 61, 71, 80, 82
Quispe Tito, Diego, 123 n

Raleg, Gualtero. *See* Raleigh, Walter
Raleigh, Walter, 41, 120–21 n
Raphael, archangel, 75, 124 n
rapto de Proserpina, El, 84

Recuerdos de la monarquía peruana, o Bosquejo de la historia de los incas, 123 n
redentor no nacido, mártir, confesor y virgen: San Ramón, El, 99
Reedy, Daniel R., 99, 127 n
Relación de las cosas de Yucatán, 23
Relación del descubrimiento y conquista de los reinos del Perú, 121 n
Reverte Bernal, Concepción, 16, 98, 101
Rimac, Juan del. *See* Vargas Ugarte, Rubén
Rojo, Grínor, 16
Rostworowski, María, 122 n
Royal Hunt of the Sun, The, 119 n
Rumiñagüi (or Rumiñahui), 100, 113–14, 128 n
runa simi [Quechua], 89

Sahagún, Bernardino de, 119 n
Sahauraura Ramos Tito Atauchi, Justo Apu, 122 n, 124 n
Sainete, Fin de Fiesta, 127 n
San Antonio Abad, seminary (Cuzco), 84–85, 89–90, 94, 126 n
San Bernardo, school (Cuzco), 89
San Francisco de Borja, school (Cuzco), 39, 89, 120 n, 125 n
San Ignacio de Loyola, university (Cuzco), 85, 89, 125 n
San Marcos, university, 122 n, 125 n
Sánchez Calderón, Cristóbal, 99
Santa Cruz Pumacallao, Basilio, 123 n
Santiago, Apostle, 64
Santo Tomás, Domingo de, 62
Sartoc, Acignio. *See* Castro, Ignacio de
Sayri Tupac, 39, 53
Scott, James C., 17
Seathiel (or Seactiel), archangel, 124 n
Shaffer, Peter, 119 n
Shelley, Kathleen, 16
Sigüenza y Góngora, Carlos de, 128 n
Sínodo quitense. Constituciones para curas de indios, 123 n
Sísara, general, 90–91, 93–95, 126 n
Solís, Diego de, 41
Soto, Hernando de, 109–10
Sucre, Antonio José de, 122 n
Sunturhuasi, 82
Symbolo Cathólico Indiano, 123 n

Tahuantinsuyu, Inca Empire, 23, 38, 41, 47, 49, 54, 68, 96, 102, 104, 108, 113, 121 n, 127 n
taqui onqoy [dance sickness], 48–49
Temple, Ella Dunbar, 122 n
Teófilo, miracle of, 59, 61
Terralla y Landa, Esteban de, 99
Tercero catecismo y exposición de la doctrina cristiana por sermones, 62
Tesoro de la lengua castellana, 86, 92
Testera, Jacobo de, 31
Thomas, Saint, 85
Tirso de Molina, 90
Tito Yupanqui, Francisco, 68
Titu Atauchi, 100, 113
Titu Cusi Yupanqui, 48, 96
Titu Cusi Yupanqui, 120 n
Todo el ingenio lo allana, 99
Toledo, Francisco de, Viceroy of Peru, 56, 96, 121 n, 122 n, 125 n
Tradiciones en salsa verde, 98
Tragedia del fin de Atahualpa, 17–18, 36, 38, 43, 49–50, 54, 56, 117, 128 n
Tupac Amaru I (last Inca), 40, 43, 56, 96, 117, 121 n
Tupac Amaru II, José Gabriel Condorcanqui, 38–41, 43, 53, 120 n
Tupac Catari, Julián Aspa, 120 n
Tupac Inca Yupanqui, 121 n

Ucu Pacha [underworld], 93
Ulloa, Antonio de, 128 n
Uriel, archangel, 124 n
Usca Paucar, 18, 58, 61, 71, 80–83
Usca Paucar, auto sacramental del Patrocinio de Nuestra Señora María en Copacabana, 17, 60–61, 68, 71, 76, 80, 83, 117–18, 122 n, 123 n

Valcárcel, Luis E., 122 n, 124 n
Valle Caviedes, Juan del, 16, 99
Valverde, Vicente de, 36, 47, 53, 113
Vargas Llosa, Mario, 88, 97
Vargas Ugarte, Rubén, 16, 90, 98, 126 n, 127 n
Vega Carpio, Lope de, 59, 90
Velasco, Luis de, viceroy, 126 n
Viaje a la América Meridional, 128 n
viaje fascinante por la América Hispana del siglo XVI, Un, 123 n
Vigote, 91, 94
Virgen de la Caridad del Cobre, 123 n
Virgin Mary, 59, 61, 68, 75, 80, 82–83, 123 n, 124 n; cult of, 61, 64, 68, 71, 75, 80
Virgin of the Rosary, 123 n

Wachtel, Nathan, 38, 48
wanka [song by women], 34

Yllescas, Inca, 114, 128 n
Yunca Nina. *See* Devil